HAL•LEONARD®

BASS PLAY-ALONG

AUDIO ACCESS INCLUDED

VOL. 56

BOB SEGER

Cover photo: Getty Images/Richard E. Aaron / Contributor

To access audio visit:
www.halleonard.com/mylibrary

Enter Code
3884-1925-3463-6363

ISBN 978-1-5400-2627-9

Visit Hal Leonard Online at
www.halleonard.com

Contact Us:
Hal Leonard
7777 West Bluemound Road
Milwaukee, WI 53213
Email: info@halleonard.com

In Europe contact:
Hal Leonard Europe Limited
42 Wigmore Street
Marylebone, London, W1U 2RN
Email: info@halleonardeurope.com

In Australia contact:
Hal Leonard Australia Pty. Ltd.
4 Lentara Court
Cheltenham, Victoria, 3192 Australia
Email: info@halleonard.com.au

Bass Notation Legend

Bass music can be notated two different ways: on a *musical staff,* and in *tablature*

THE MUSICAL STAFF shows pitches and rhythms and is divided by bar lines into measures. Pitches are named after the first seven letters of the alphabet.

TABLATURE graphically represents the bass fingerboard. Each horizontal line represents a string, and each number represents a fret.

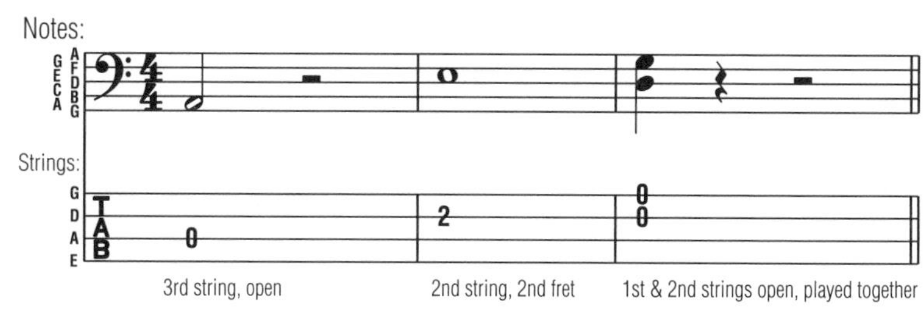

HAMMER-ON: Strike the first (lower) note with one finger, then sound the higher note (on the same string) with another finger by fretting it without picking.

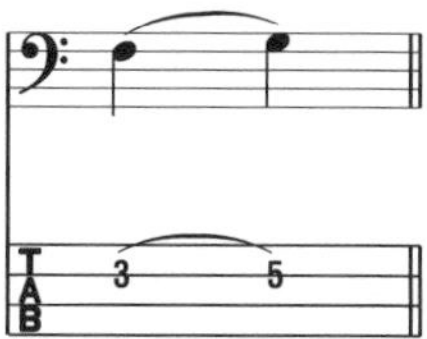

PULL-OFF: Place both fingers on the notes to be sounded. Strike the first note and without picking, pull the finger off to sound the second (lower) note.

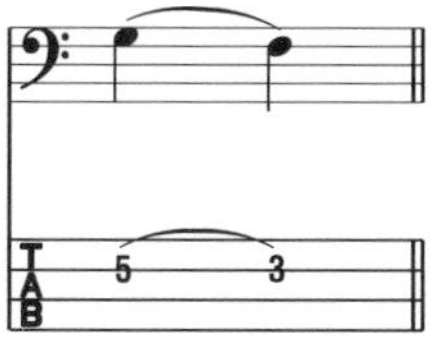

LEGATO SLIDE: Strike the first note and then slide the same fret-hand finger up or down to the second note. The second note is not struck.

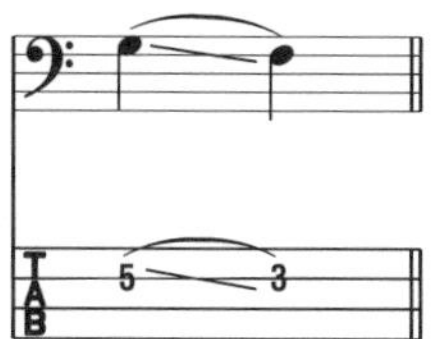

SHIFT SLIDE: Same as legato slide, except the second note is struck.

TRILL: Very rapidly alternate between the notes indicated by continuously hammering on and pulling off.

TREMOLO PICKING: The note is picked as rapidly and continuously as possible.

VIBRATO: The string is vibrated by rapidly bending and releasing the note with the fretting hand.

SHAKE: Using one finger, rapidly alternate between two notes on one string by sliding either a half-step above or below.

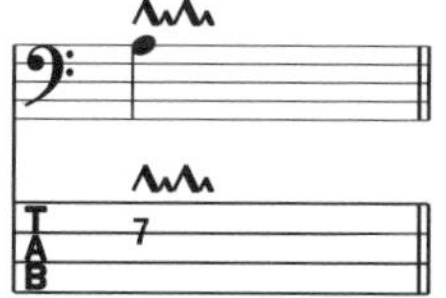

NATURAL HARMONIC: Strike the note while the fret hand lightly touches the string directly over the fret indicated.

MUFFLED STRINGS: A percussive sound is produced by laying the fret hand across the string(s) without depressing them and striking them with the pick hand.

BEND: Strike the note and bend up the interval shown.

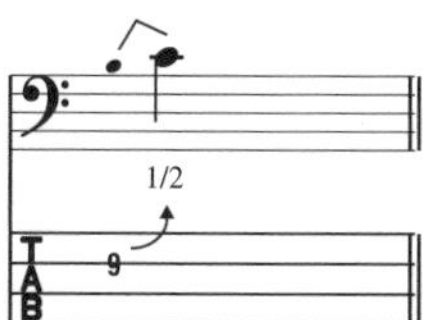

BEND AND RELEASE: Strike the note and bend up as indicated, then release back to the original note. Only the first note is struck.

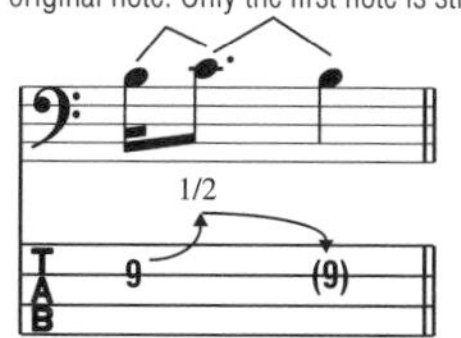

RIGHT-HAND TAP: Hammer ("tap") the fret indicated with the "pick-hand" index or middle finger and pull off to the note fretted by the fret hand.

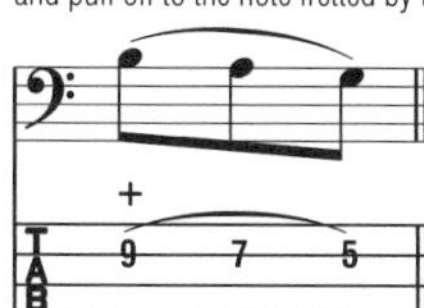

LEFT-HAND TAP: Hammer ("tap") the fret indicated with the "fret-hand" index or middle finger.

SLAP: Strike ("slap") string with right-hand thumb.

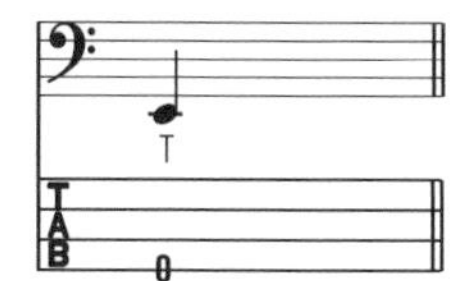

POP: Snap ("pop") string with right-hand index or middle finger.

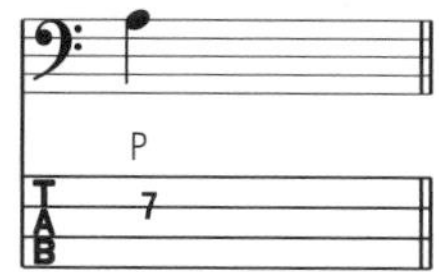

Additional Musical Definitions

(accent) • Accentuate note (play it louder)

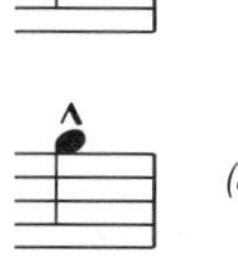

(accent) • Accentuate note with great intensity

(staccato) • Play the note short

D.S. al Coda • Go back to the sign (𝄋), then play until the measure marked ***"To Coda"***, then skip to the section labelled ***"Coda."***

Fill • Label used to identify a brief pattern which is to be inserted into the arrangement.

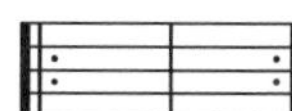

• Repeat measures between signs.

• When a repeated section has different endings, play the first ending only the first time and the second ending only the second time.

Against the Wind

Words and Music by Bob Seger

G
Bm
and the se-crets that we shared,
the moun - tains that we moved;
C
G
caught like a wild - fire out of con-trol,
till there was
C
D
noth - in' left to burn and noth - in' left to prove.
And I re -
Pre-Chorus
Em
D
G
Em
C
mem - ber what she said to me,
how she swore that it nev - er would end.
See additional lyrics

G
Em
D
C
I re - mem - ber how she held me, oh, so tight.
To Coda
D
Wish I did - n't know now what I did - n't know then.
Chorus
G
Bm
C
A - gainst the wind,
we were run - nin' a - gainst the wind.
G
C
Bm
Am
C
We were young and strong, we were run - nin' a - gainst the

G
wind.
Verse
G
2. And the years rolled slow-ly past,
Bm
and I found my-self a-lone.
C
Sur-round-ed by strang-ers I thought were
G
my friends.
D
I found my-self fur-ther and fur-ther
C
from my home and I,
G
guess I lost my way.

Bm
There were oh so man - y roads. I was a

C G C
liv - in' to run and run - nin' to live. Nev - er wor - ried a - bout pay - in' or e - ven how

Pre-Chorus
D Em D
much I owed. Mov - ing eight miles a min - ute for months at a

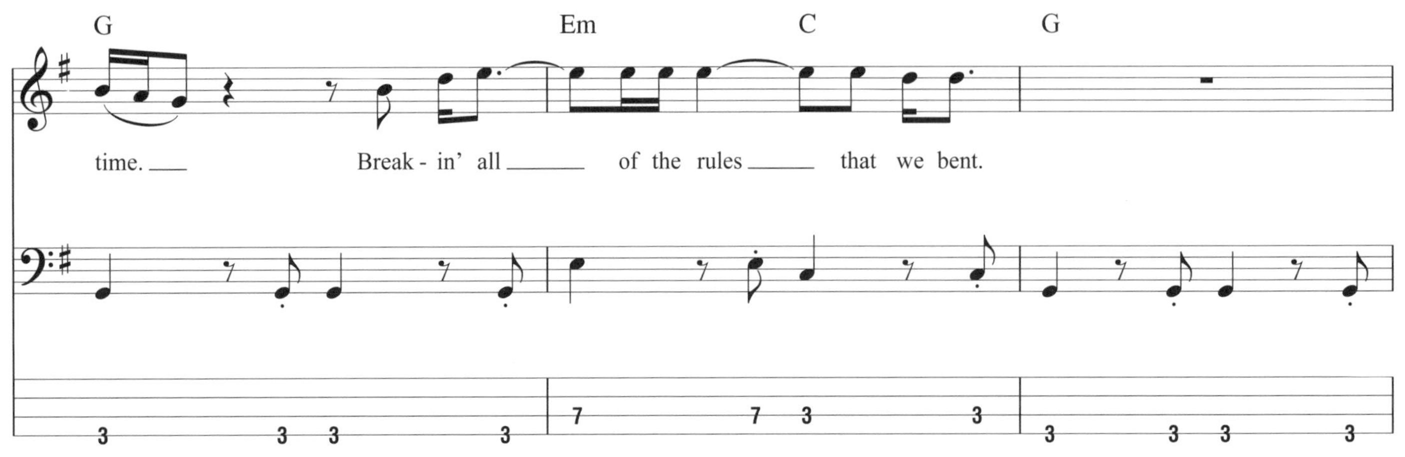
G Em C G
time. Break - in' all of the rules that we bent.

Em D C
I be-gan to find my-self search-in',
search-in' for shel-ter a-gain
D
and a-gain.
Chorus
G Bm
A-gainst the wind,
C G C Bm
lit-tle some-thin' a-gainst the wind.
I found my-self seek-ing shel-
Am C G
-ter a-gainst the wind.

Piano Solo
G
5 5 5
5 5 7 7 5 7
3 3 3 5
3 3 3 5 3

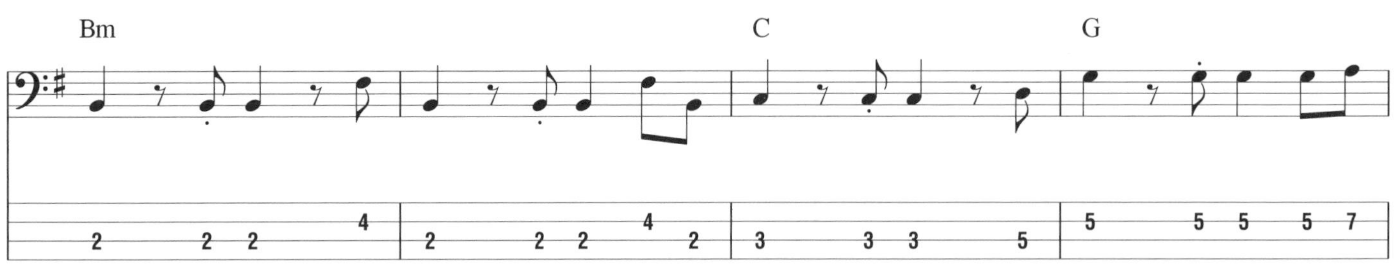
Bm
C
G
2 2 2 4
2 2 2 4 2
3 3 3 5
5 5 5 5 7

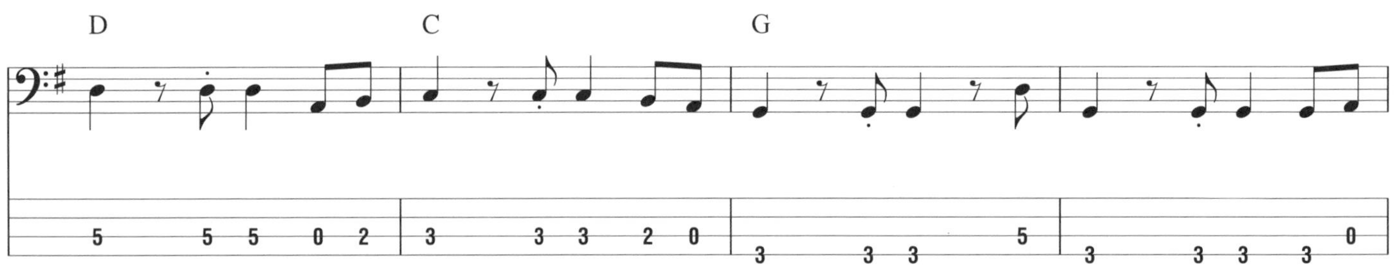
D
C
G
5 5 5 0 2
3 3 3 2 0
3 3 3 5
3 3 3 3 0

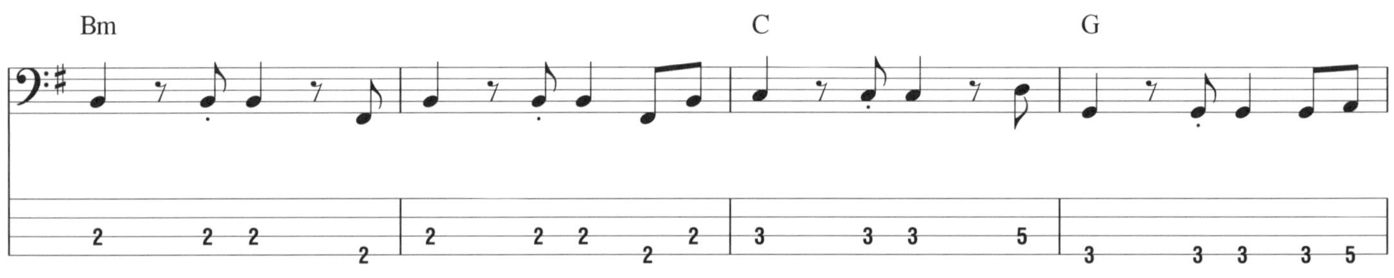
Bm
C
G
2 2 2 2
2 2 2 2 2
3 3 3 5
3 3 3 3 5

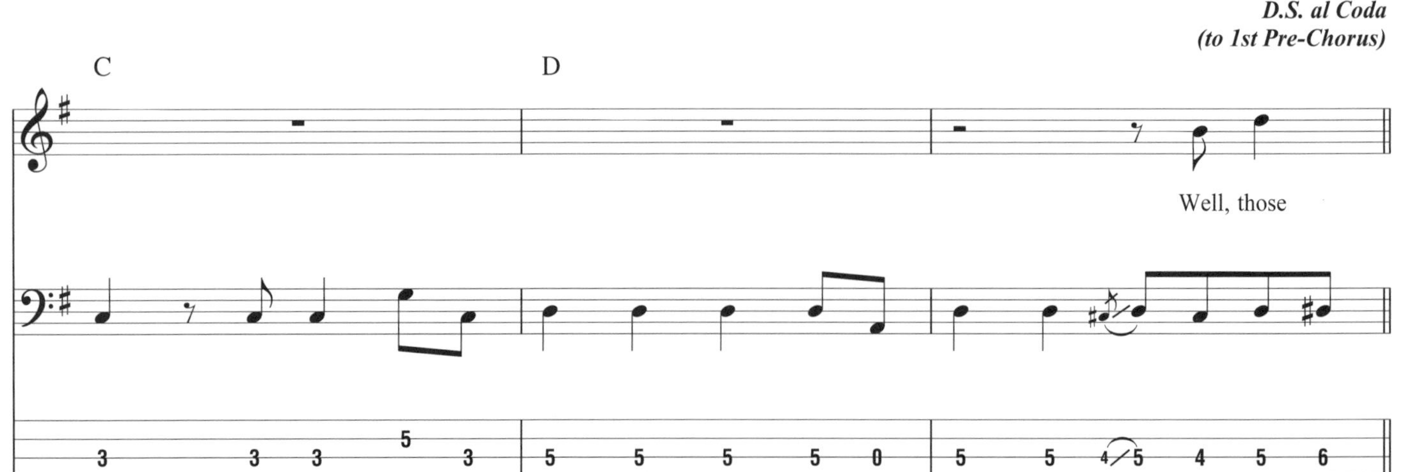
D.S. al Coda
(to 1st Pre-Chorus)
C
D
Well, those
3 3 3 5 3
5 5 5 5 0
5 5 4 5 4 5 6

Coda
Chorus
G
Bm
what to leave out.
A - gainst the wind.
C
G
I'm still run - nin' a - gainst the wind.
I'm
C
Bm
Am
C
G
old - er now, but still run - nin' a - gainst the wind.
C
Bm
D
Well, I'm old - er now and still run - nin'

C
a - gainst the wind.
A - gainst the
G
wind.
A - gainst the wind.
w/ Lead Voc. ad lib., till fade
C
A - gainst the wind.
G
A - gainst the
Outro
C
wind.
A - gainst the wind.
G

C
A - gainst
the
wind.
A - gainst
the
G
wind.
C
A - gainst
the
wind.
G
A - gainst
the
wind.
A - gainst
the
C
wind.
G
A - gainst
the
wind.

Additional Lyrics

Pre-Chorus Well, those drifter's days are past me now.
I've got so much more to think about.
Deadlines and commitments;
What to leave in, what to leave out.

Her Strut

Words and Music by Bob Seger

Tune down 1/2 step:
(low to high) E♭-A♭-D♭-G♭

Intro

Moderate Rock  **= 115**

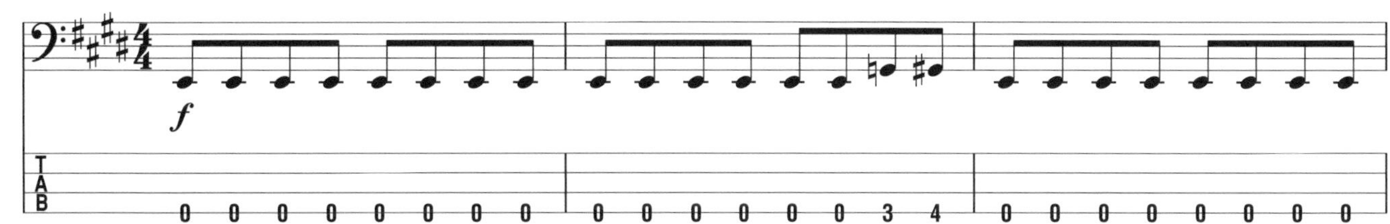

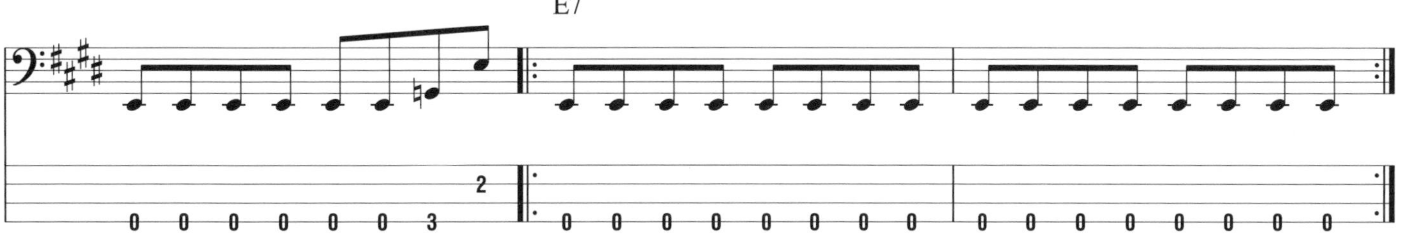

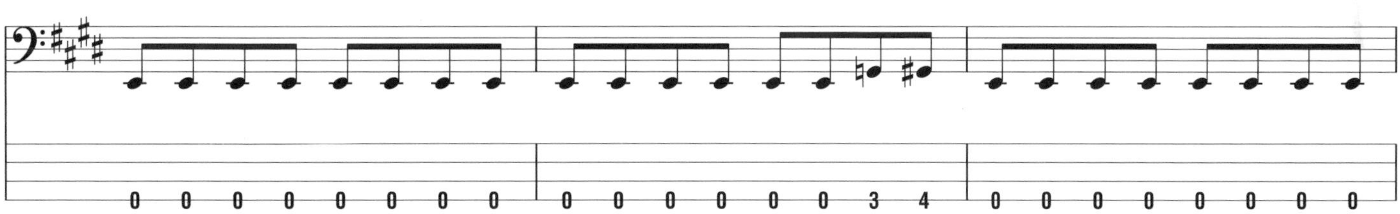

Verse

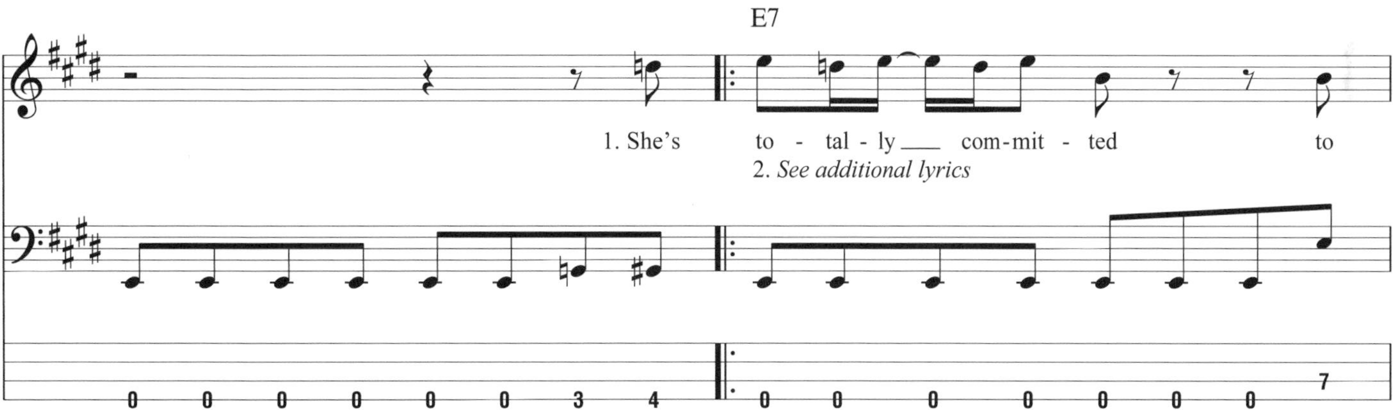

She gives them quite a bat - tle, all
that they can han - dle; she'll bruise some, she'll hurt some, too.
Chorus
A5
C5
But, oh,
Oh,
they love to watch her
E
A5
strut.
Oh,
1/4

2nd time, substitute Fill 1
C5
B5
N.C.
they do respect her but they love to watch her
they'll kill to make the cut. They love to watch her
Interlude
E7
strut. Uh!
strut. Ah!
Oh, yeah.
1.
Oh.
2.
2. Some -
Love to watch.
Fill 1

Guitar Solo
E7
Watch her strut, now.
1.
2.
1/4
Chorus
A5
C5
E5
Oh, ___
they love ___ to watch her
strut.
G5
F#5 F5 E5
A5
C5
Oh, ___
they do ___ re - spect _ her but _

Interlude
B5
N.C.
E7
they love to watch her strut. Mm.
Al - right.
Ah.
let ring
Love her strut.
Mm, hmm.
Love to, love to,
Outro
E7
love to watch her strut. Mm.

Love _ to watch her strut.
Al - right.
They love her
strut.
Mm.
Love a la - dy's strut.
Mm.

Additional Lyrics

2. Sometimes they'll want to leave her, just give up and leave her,
But they would never play that scene.
In spite of all her talking, once she starts in walking,
The lady will be all they ever dreamed.

Fire Lake

Words and Music by Bob Seger

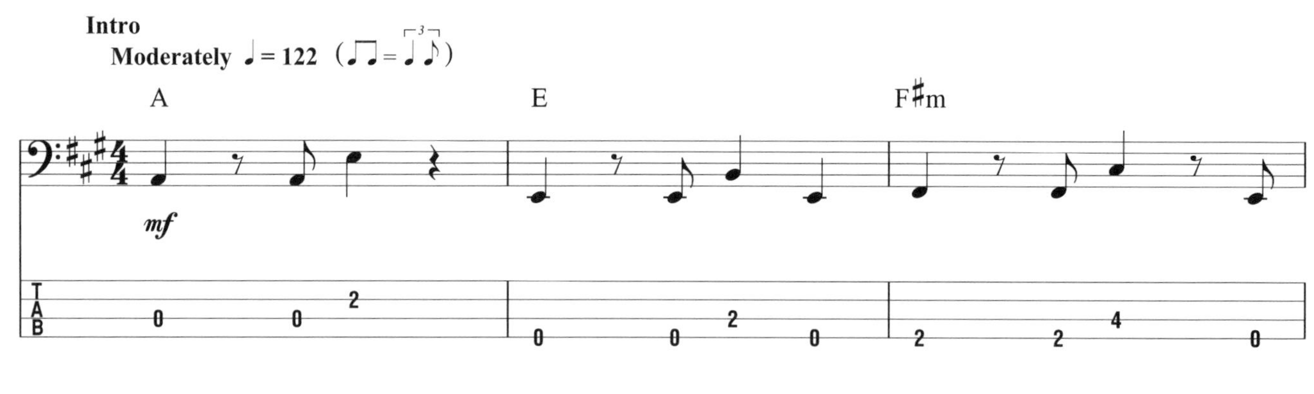

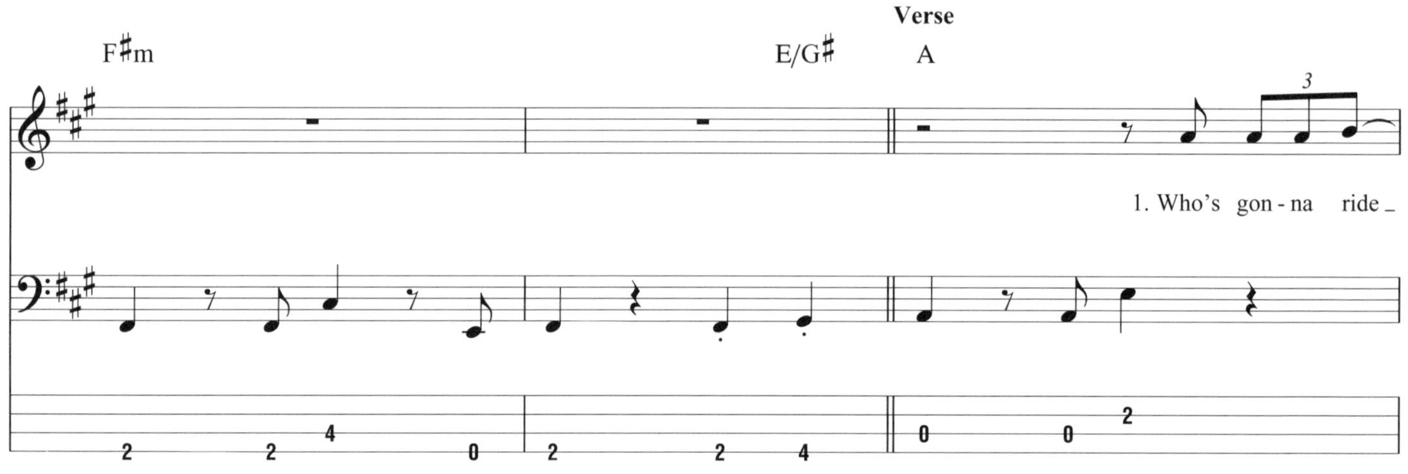

A
E
F♯m
Who's gon-na make that first mis - take?
E/G♯
A
E
Who wants to wear those gyp - sy leath-ers?
F♯m
E/G♯
A
All the way
E
F♯m
E/G♯
to Fi - re Lake.

Verse
A
E
F♯m
2. Who wants to break the news about Uncle Joe?
E/G♯
A
E
You re-mem-ber Un-cle Joe; he was the one a-fraid to cut the cake.
F♯m
E/G♯
A
Who wants to
E
F♯m
E/G♯
tell poor Aunt Sar-ah,

A
E
F♯m
Joe has run off to Fi - re Lake?
E/G♯
A
E
Joe has run off to Fi - re Lake.
F♯m
E
Bridge
D
Who wants to brave those
C♯m
F♯m
bronze beau - ties ly - ing in the sun, with their

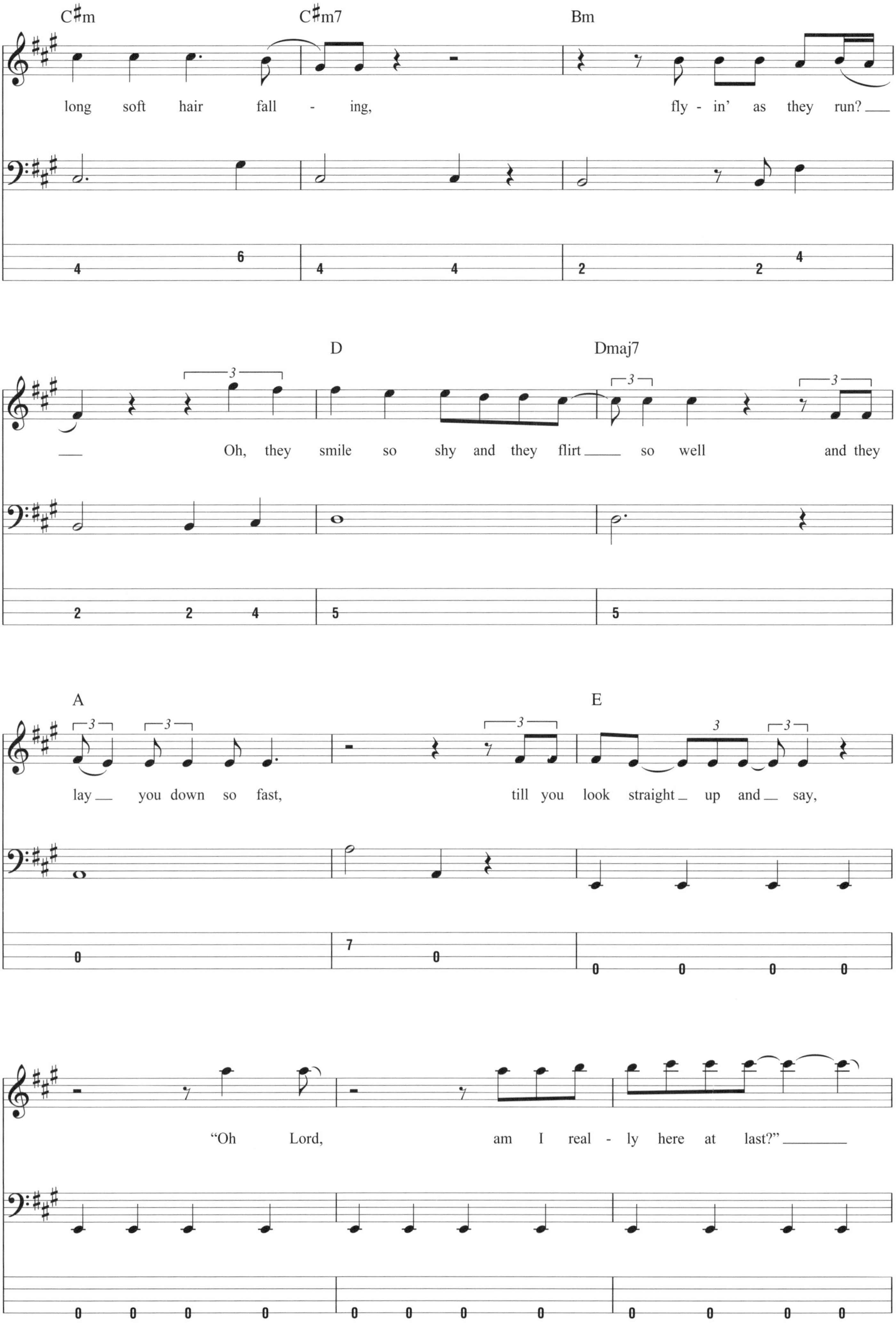

C♯m
C♯m7
Bm
long soft hair fall - ing,
fly - in' as they run?
D
Dmaj7
Oh, they smile so shy and they flirt so well and they
A
E
lay you down so fast,
till you look straight up and say,
"Oh Lord, am I real - ly here at last?"

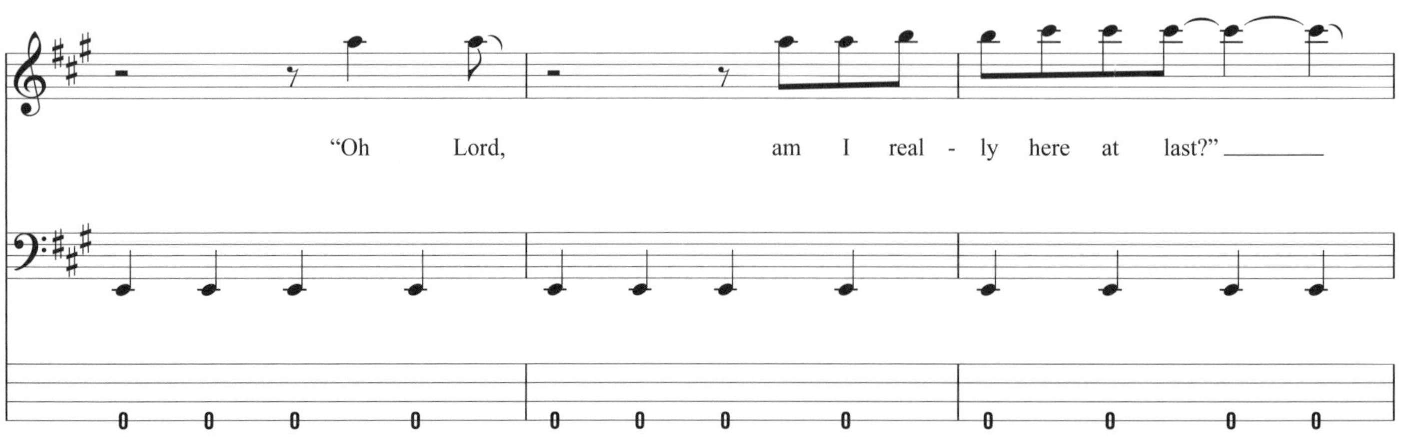

Verse
A
E
3. Who wants to play those eights_ and ac - es?
F♯m
E/G♯
A
Who wants a
E
F♯m
E/G♯
raise,_ who needs a stake?___
A
E
F♯m
Who wants to take that long shot gam - ble, ha,___

E/G♯
A
E
and head out to Fi - re Lake?
F♯m
Outro
E/G♯
A
Voc. Fig. 1
And head out.
(Who wants to
w/ Lead Voc. ad lib, till fade
E
F♯m
E/G♯
go to Fi - re Lake?
A
E
F♯m
E/G♯
End Voc. Fig. 1
Who wants to go to Fi - re Lake?

Bkgd. Voc.: w/ Voc. Fig. 1, till fade
A
E
F♯m
E/G♯
Begin fade
Fade out

Hollywood Nights

Words and Music by Bob Seger

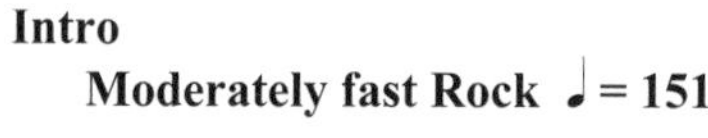

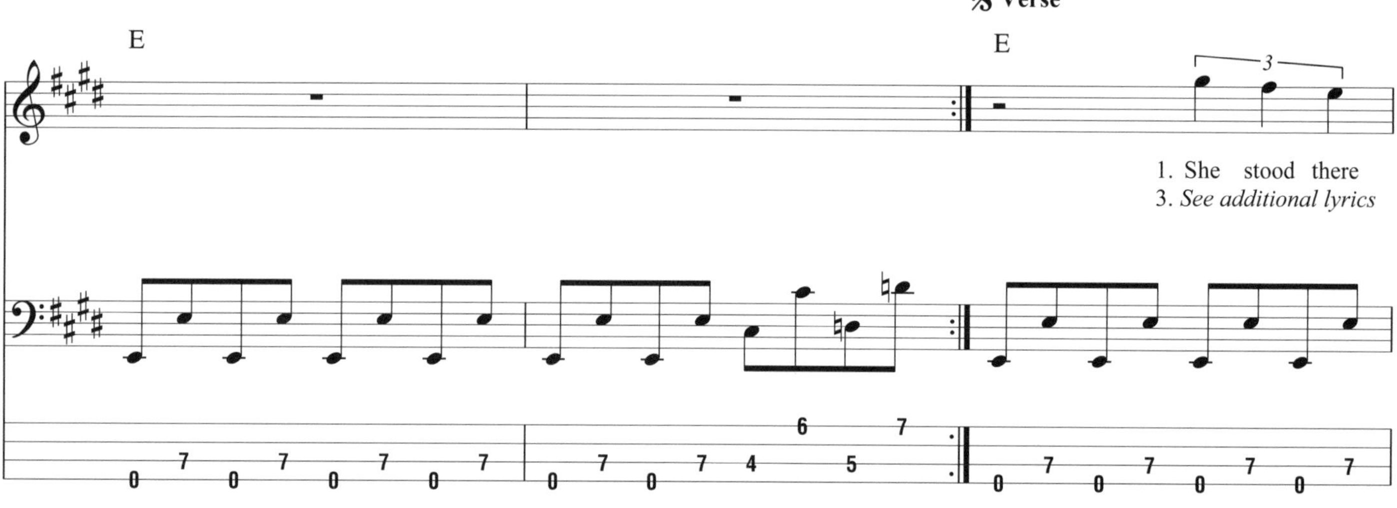

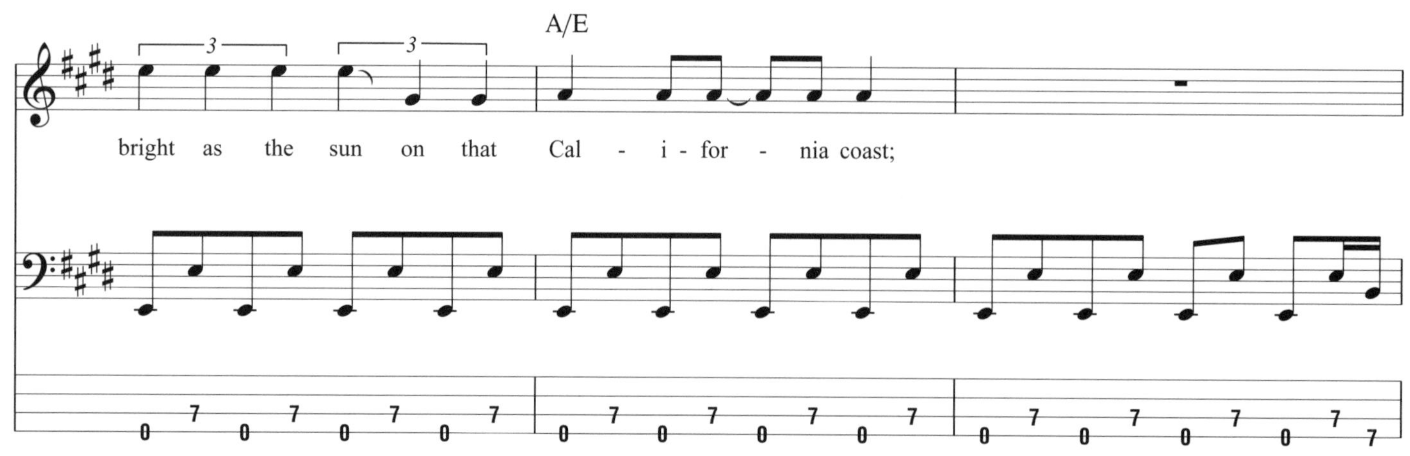

D/E
E
he was a Mid - west - ern boy on his own.
She looked at him with those soft eyes, so
A/E
D/E
in - no - cent and blue.
He knew right
E
then he was too far from home.

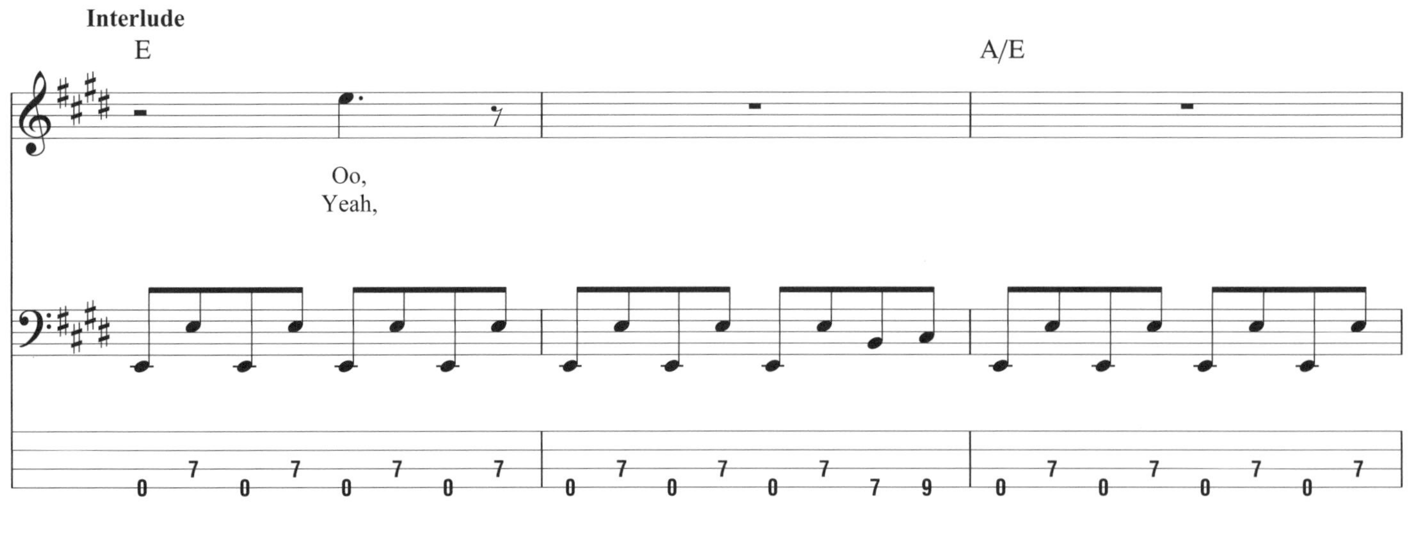
Interlude
E
A/E
Oo,
Yeah,

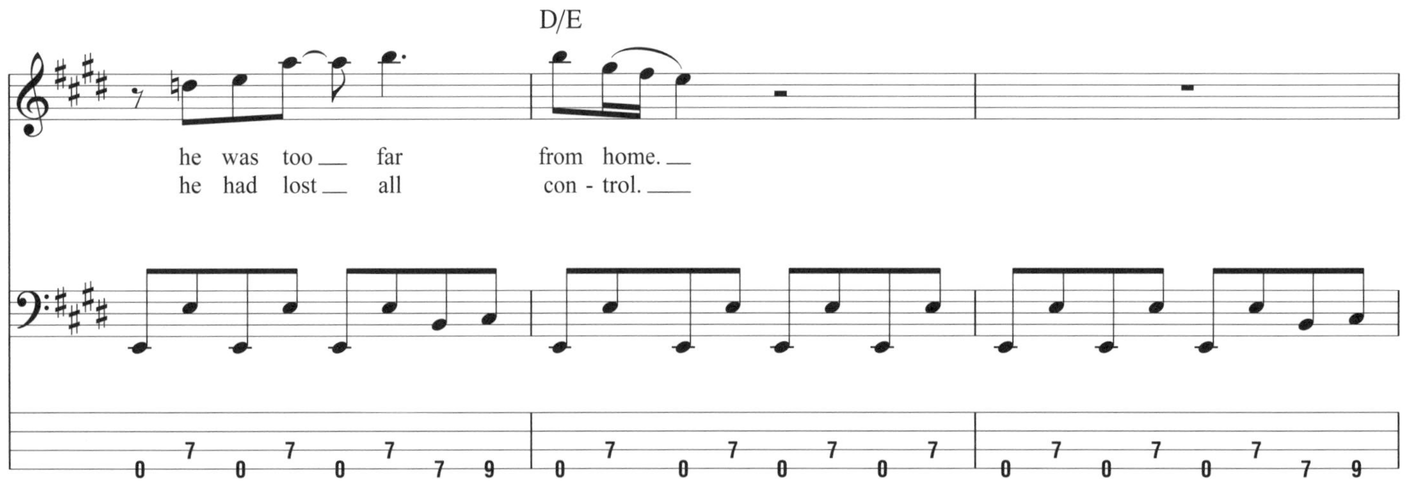
D/E
he was too far from home.
he had lost all con - trol.

2nd time, substitute Fill 1
Verse
E
E
2. She took his
4. See additional lyrics

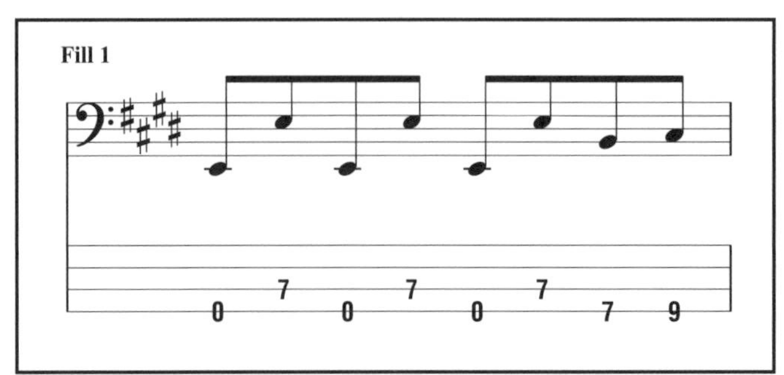
Fill 1

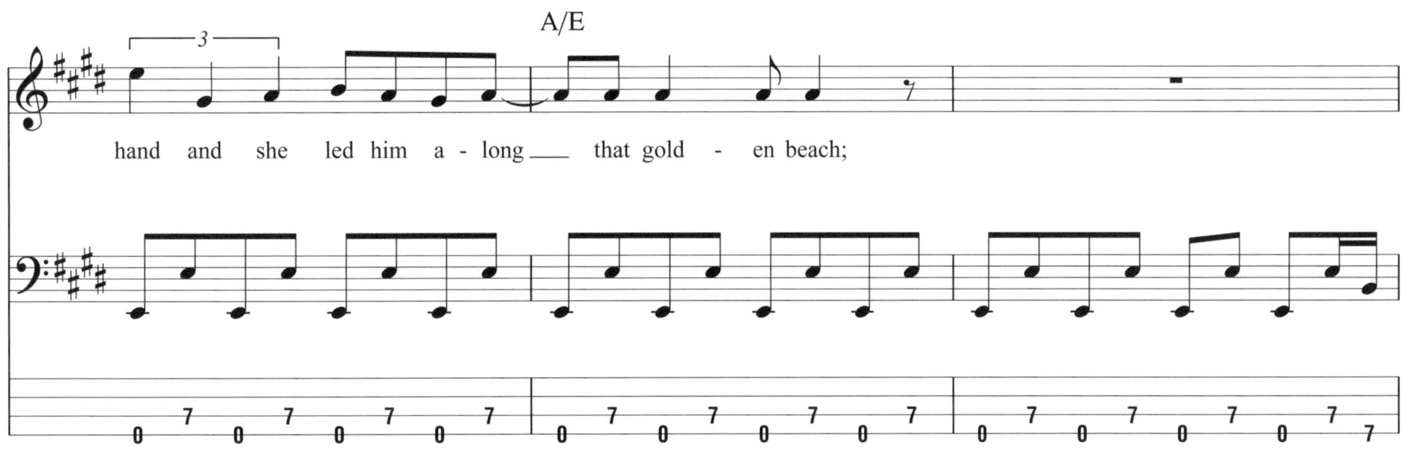
A/E
hand and she led him a - long that gold - en beach;
0 7 0 7 0 7 0 7
0 7 0 7 0 7 0 7
0 7 0 7 0 7 0 7 7

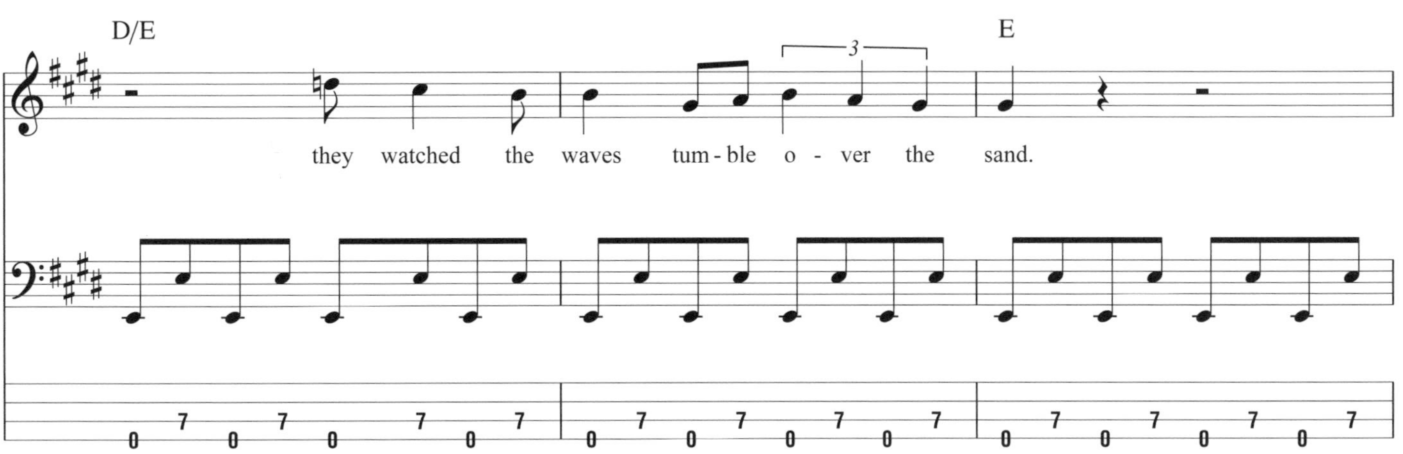
D/E
E
they watched the waves tum - ble o - ver the sand.
0 7 0 7 0 7 0 7
0 7 0 7 0 7 0 7
0 7 0 7 0 7 0 7

2nd time, substitute Fill 2
They drove for miles and miles up those
0 7 0 7 0 7 5 7
0 7 0 7 0 7 0 7
0 7 0 7 0 7 0 7 7

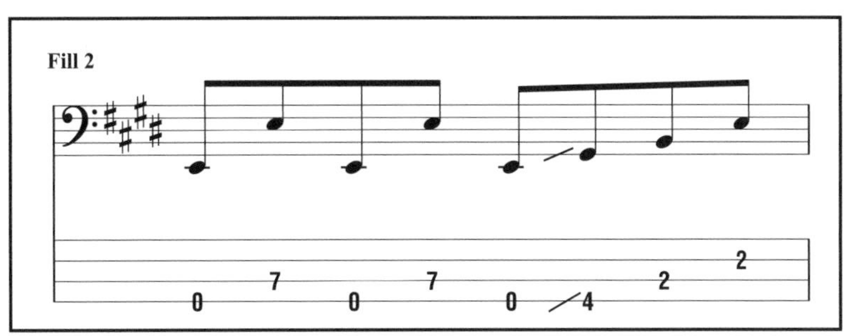
Fill 2
0 7 0 7 0 4 2 2

2nd time, substitute Fill 1
A/E
D/E
twist-ing, turn-ing roads;
high-er and
To Coda
E
high-er and high-er they climbed.
And those Hol-
Chorus
E
A/E
-ly-wood nights
in those Hol-ly-wood hills.
D/E
She was look-ing so right
in her dia-

E
- monds and frills.
All those big city - y nights
A/E
in those high, roll - ing hills;
a -
D/E
bove all the lights,
she had all of the skills.
E
Bridge
D
Ah.

A
E
Yeah!
A/E
E
Ow.
D.S. al Coda
Mm.
Coda
Chorus
E
A/E
- ly - wood nights,
in those Hol - ly-wood hills.

D/E
It was look - ing so right, it was giv -
E
- ing him chills.
In those big cit - y nights,
A/E
in those high, roll - ing hills; a -
D/E
bove all the lights
E
with a pas - sion that kills.

In those Hol - ly-wood nights, in those Hol -
A/E
D/E
- ly - wood hills. She was look - in' so right
E
in her dia - monds and frills. All those big
city lights in those high, roll - ing hills.
A/E

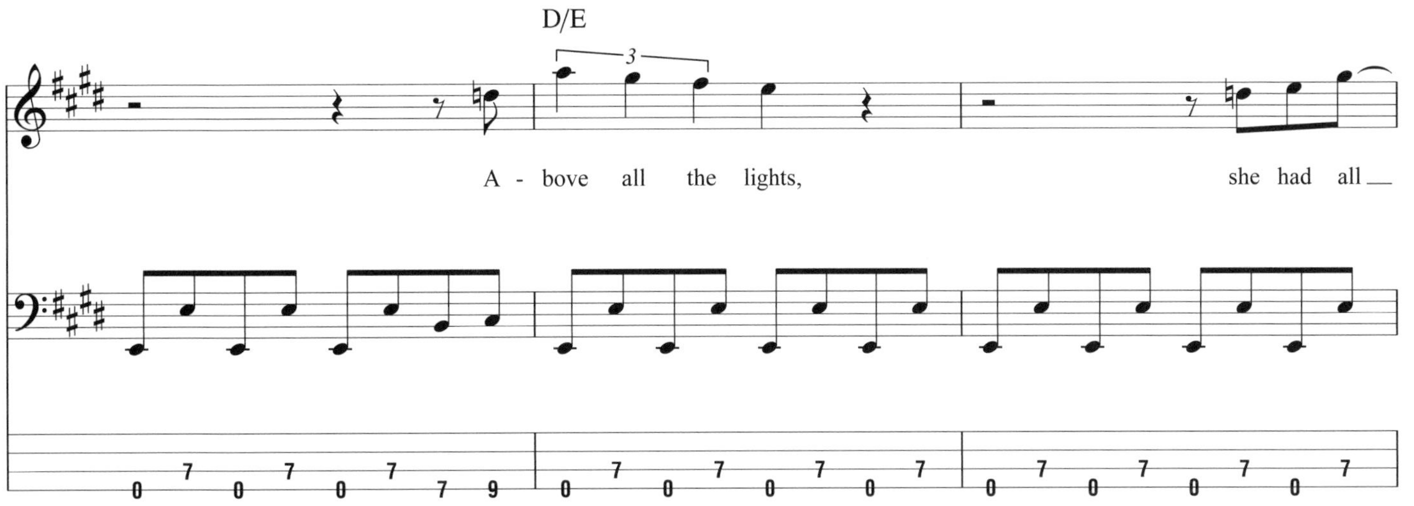
D/E
3
A - bove all the lights, she had all
7 7 7 7 9
0 0 0 7 9
7 7 7 7
0 0 0 0
7 7 7 7
0 0 0 0

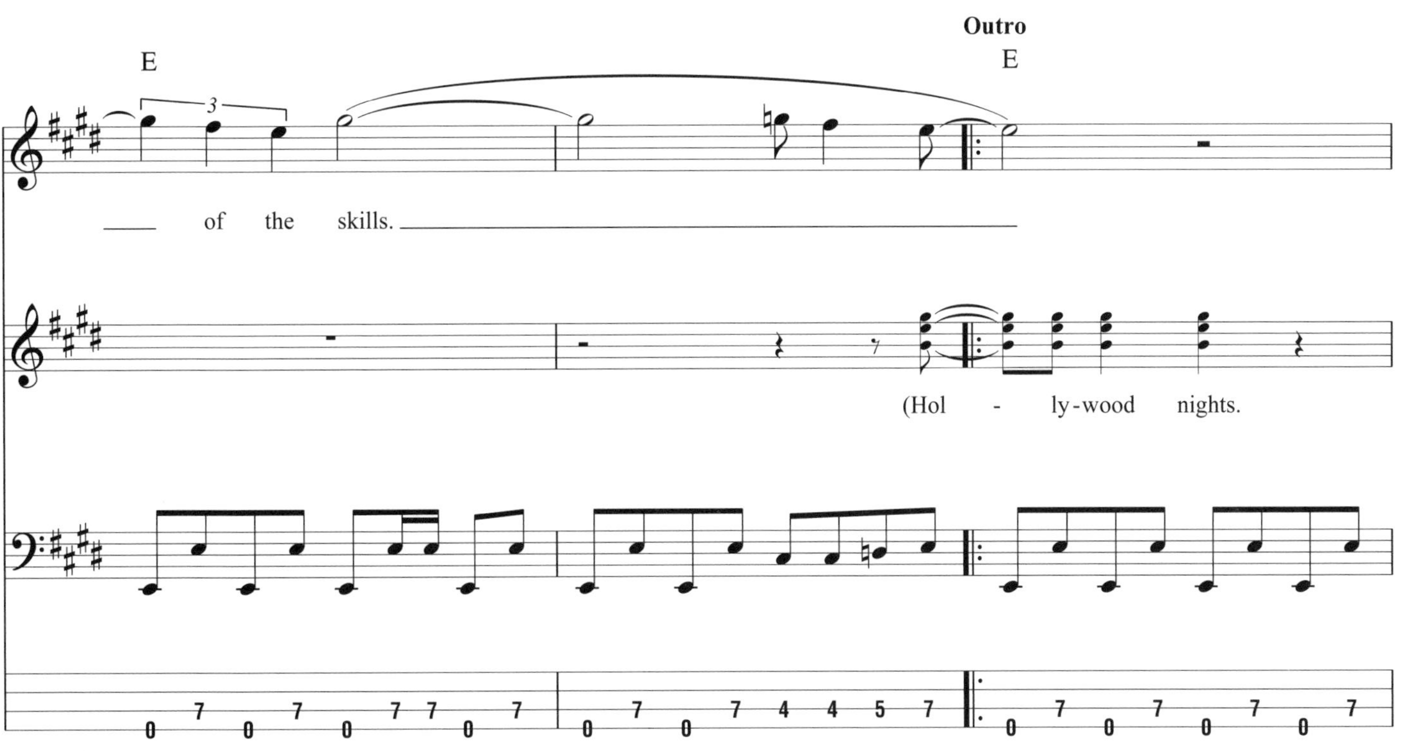
Outro
E
E
3
of the skills.
(Hol - ly-wood nights.
7 7 7 7 7
0 0 0 0
7 7 4 4 5 7
0 0
7 7 7 7
0 0 0 0

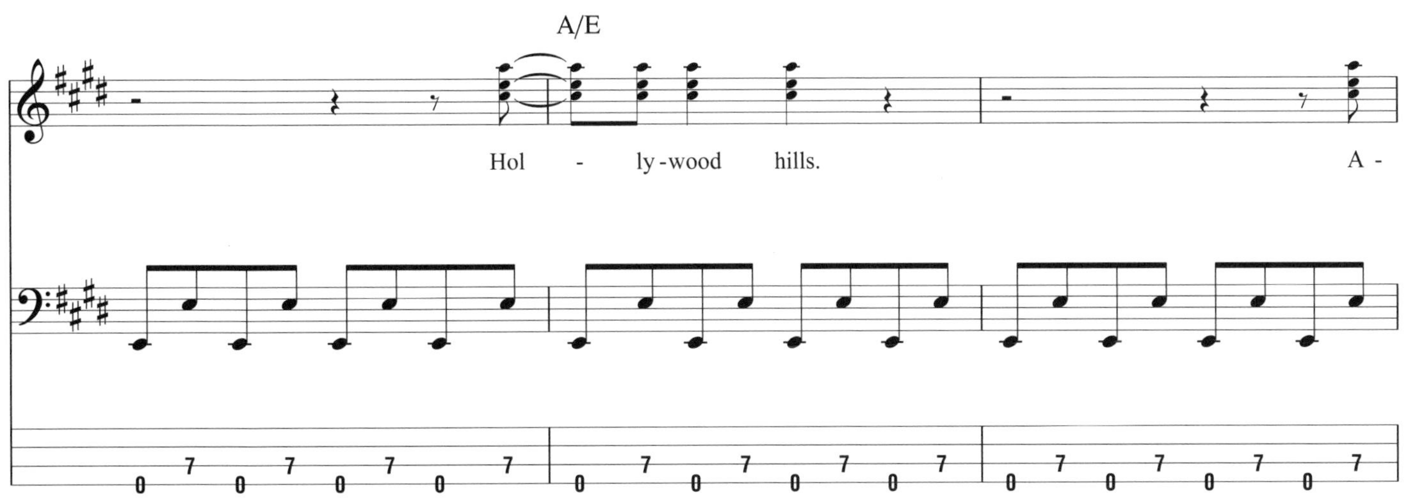
A/E
Hol - ly-wood hills. A -
7 7 7 7
0 0 0 0
7 7 7 7
0 0 0 0
7 7 7 7
0 0 0 0

Additional Lyrics

3. He'd headed west 'cause he felt that a change would do him good.
See some old friends; good for the soul.
She had been born with a face that would let her get her way.
He saw that face and he lost all control.

4. Night after night and day after day, it went on and on.
Then came that morning he woke up alone.
He spent all night staring down at the lights of L.A.,
Wondering if he could ever go home.

Night Moves

Words and Music by Bob Seger

G♭
D♭
G♭
way up firm and high.
Verse
A♭
G♭
D♭
Out past the corn - fields, where the woods got heav - y;
out in the back seat of my six -
G♭
A♭
G♭
D♭
ty Chev - y.
Work - in' on mys - t'ries with - out any - y clues.
Chorus
E♭
Fm
E♭
D♭
Work - in' on our night moves,

Eb
Fm
Eb
Db
Eb
try'n' to make some front page, drive-in news.
Work-in' on our
To Coda
Fm
Eb
Db
Dbmaj7
Ab
night moves,
in the sum-mer-time.
Gb
Db
Gb
Mm,
Ab
Gb
Db
in the sweet
sum-mer-time.

Verse
G♭
A♭
3
3. We weren't in love, oh, no, far from it.
G♭ D♭
We weren't search - in' for some_ pie - in - the - sky sum - mit.
G♭
A♭
We were_ just young and rest - less and bored;_____
G♭ D♭
liv - in' by the sword.___
G♭
A♭
And we'd steal a - way ev - 'ry chance we could,
G♭ D♭

Gb Ab
to the back room, to the al-ley, or the trust-y woods.
I used her, she used me, but nei-
D.S. al Coda
Gb Db Eb
- ther one cared;
we were get-tin' our share.
Work-in' on our
Coda
Ab Gb Db
Mm,
and it was sum-mer-time.
Gb Ab
Mm,
sweet,

Interlude

Bridge

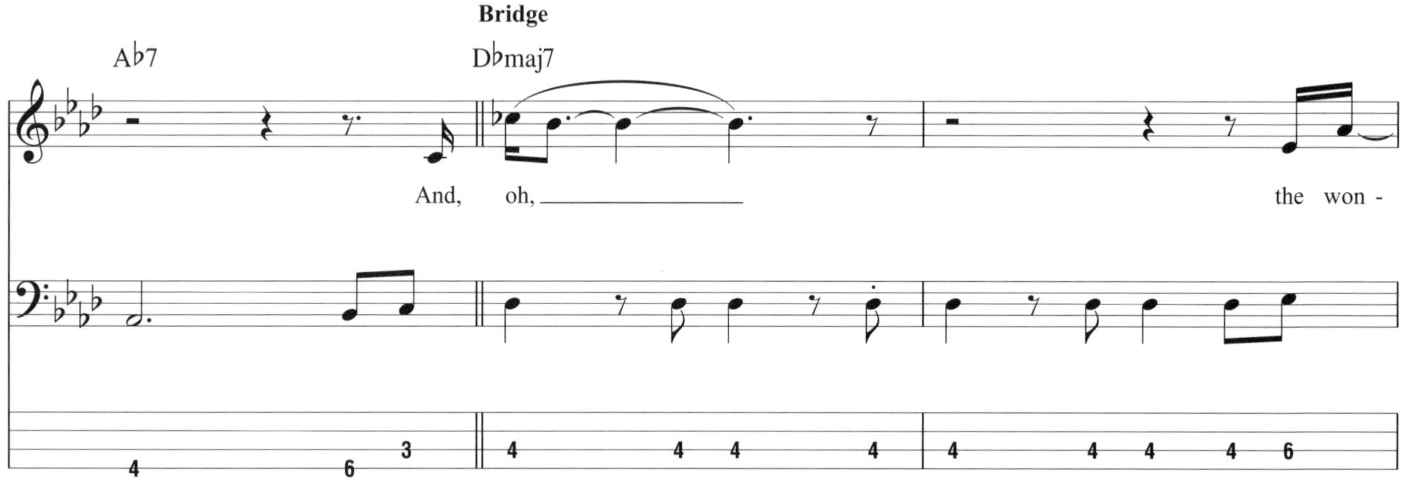

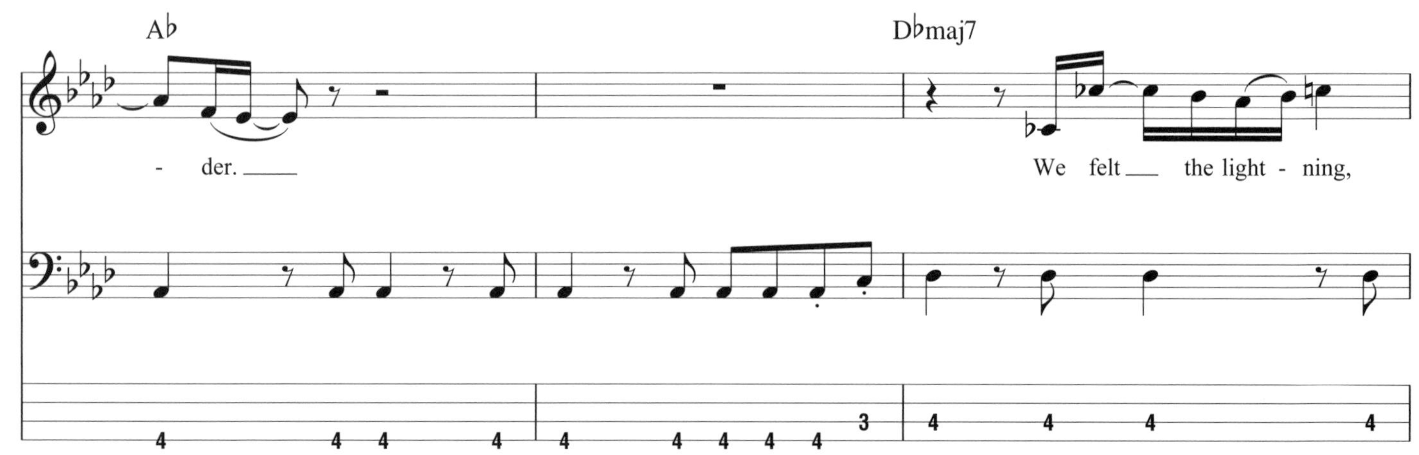

G♭
yeah, _ and we wait - ed on _ the thun - der,
E♭
Slower ♩ = 76
A♭
wait - ing on the thun - der. _
Verse
Free time
A♭
D♭maj7
4. I a - woke last night to the sound of thun - der. How far off, I sat and won - dered.
A♭
D♭maj7
Start - ed hum - ming a song from nine - teen - six - ty - two. _ Ain't it fun - ny how _ the night

Fm
Db
Fm
moves
when you just don't seem to have as much to lose?
1
4
1
Db
Fm
Db
Dbmaj7
Strange how the night moves
4
1
4
4
Interlude
Moderately ♩ = 118
Bass tacet
Ab
Ab
with au - tumn clos - ing in.
(4)
Gb
Db
Gb
Mm.
Ab
Gb
Db
Gb
Night moves.
Mm.

Outro
w/ Lead Voc. ad lib.
1.-7.
A♭
G♭ D♭
G♭
(Night moves.
Night moves.)
8.
Fm
Oo, oo.
Cm
B♭m
Ah, yeah, yeah, yeah, yeah.
Ah,
D♭
A♭
ah.
I re-mem-ber, I re-mem - ber.

Mainstreet

Words and Music by Bob Seger

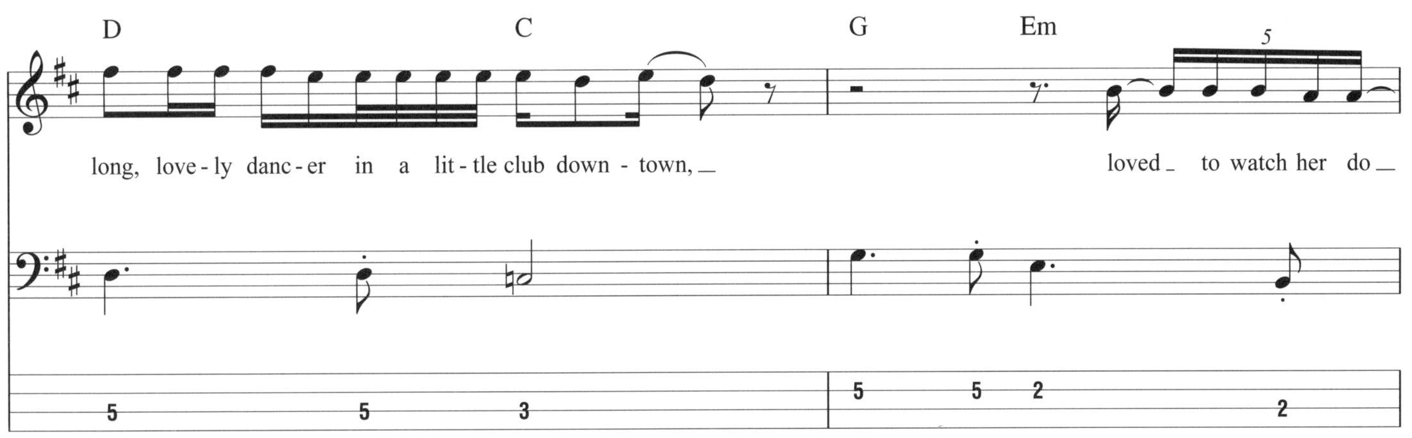
D C G Em
5
long, love-ly danc-er in a lit-tle club down-town,
loved to watch her do

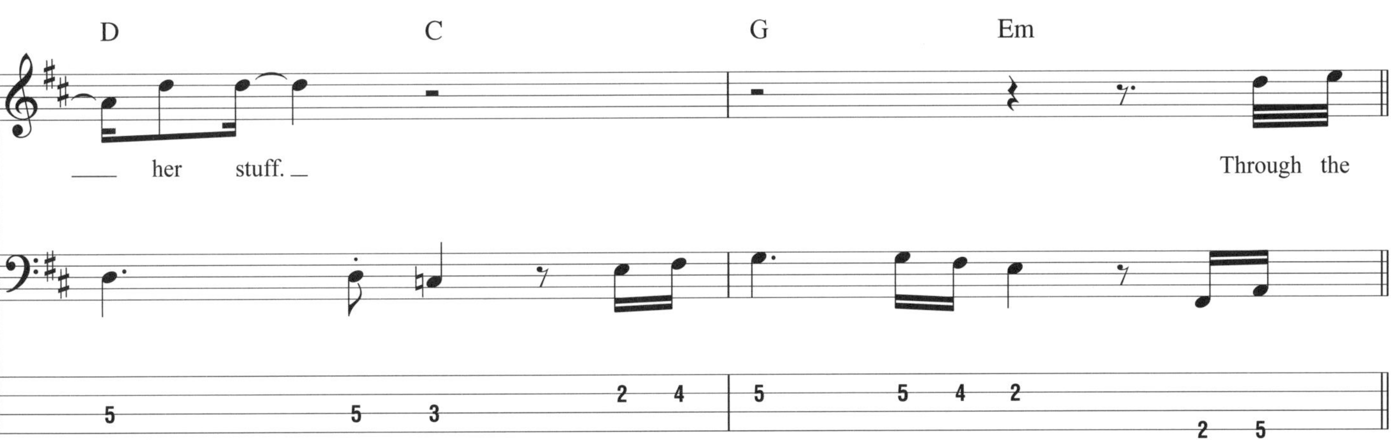
D C G Em
her stuff.
Through the

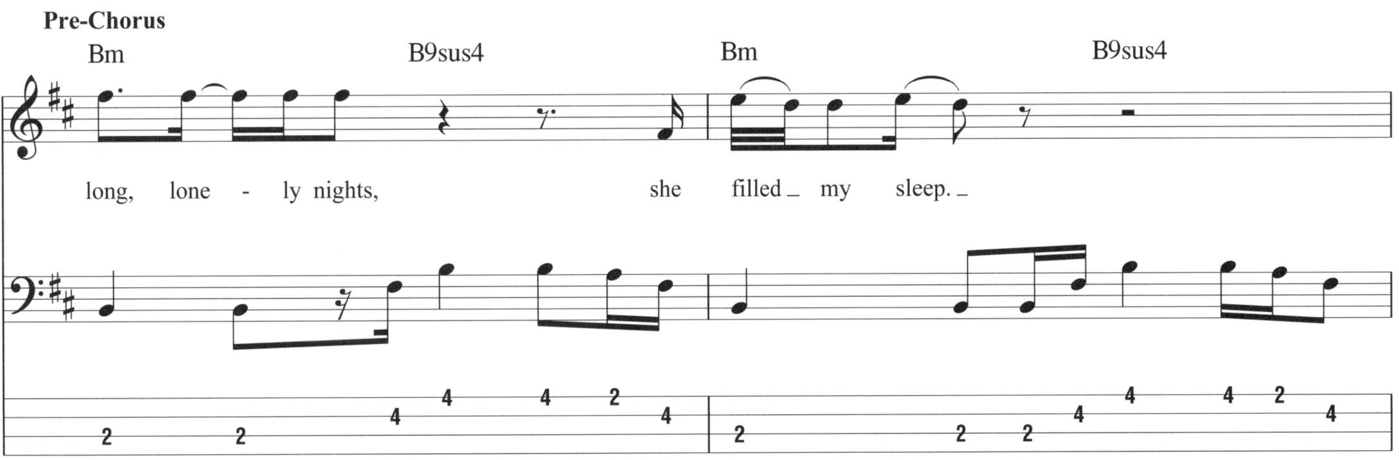
Pre-Chorus
Bm B9sus4 Bm B9sus4
long, lone-ly nights,
she filled my sleep.

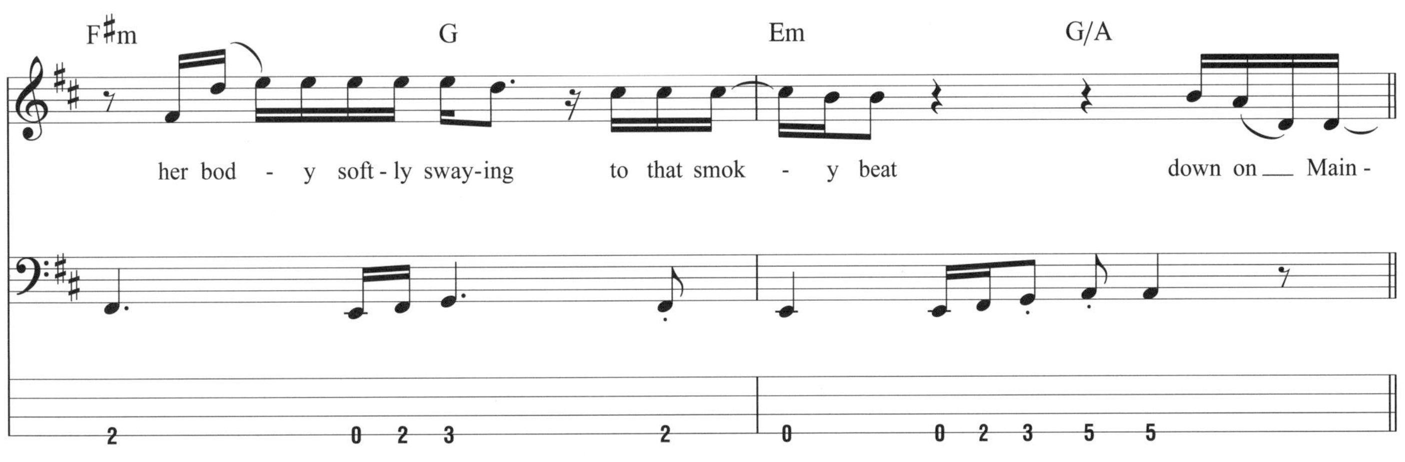
F#m G Em G/A
her bod-y soft-ly sway-ing to that smok-y beat
down on Main-

Chorus
D
C
G
Em
- street.
Down on Main -
D
C
G
Em
- street.
2. In the
Verse
D
C
G
Em
pool halls, the hus - tlers and the los - ers, used to watch 'em through
D
C
G
Em
the glass.
Well, I'd

D
C
G
Em
stand out - side at clos - ing time,
just to watch her
5 5 3 2 4 5 5 2 2 2

D
C
G
Em
walk on past.
5 5 3 2 4 5 5 4 2 2 5 2

Pre-Chorus
Bm
B9sus4
Bm
B9sus4
3
Un - like all the oth - er la - dies, she looked so young and sweet, as she
2 2 4 4 4 4 2 4 2 2 4 4 4 4 2 4

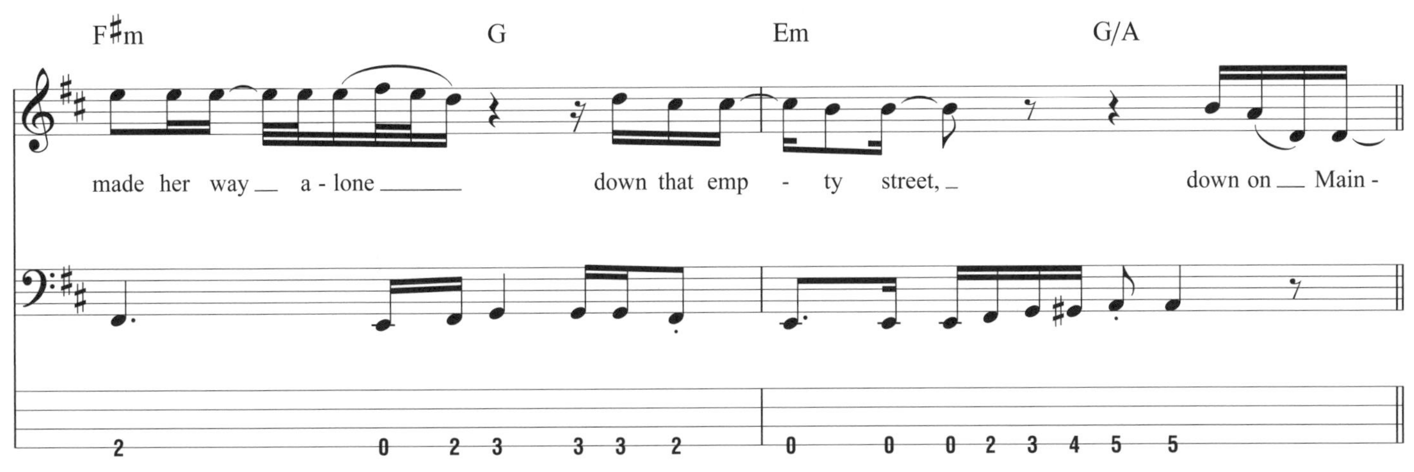
F♯m
G
Em
G/A
made her way a - lone down that emp - ty street, down on Main -
2 0 2 3 3 3 2 0 0 0 2 3 4 5 5

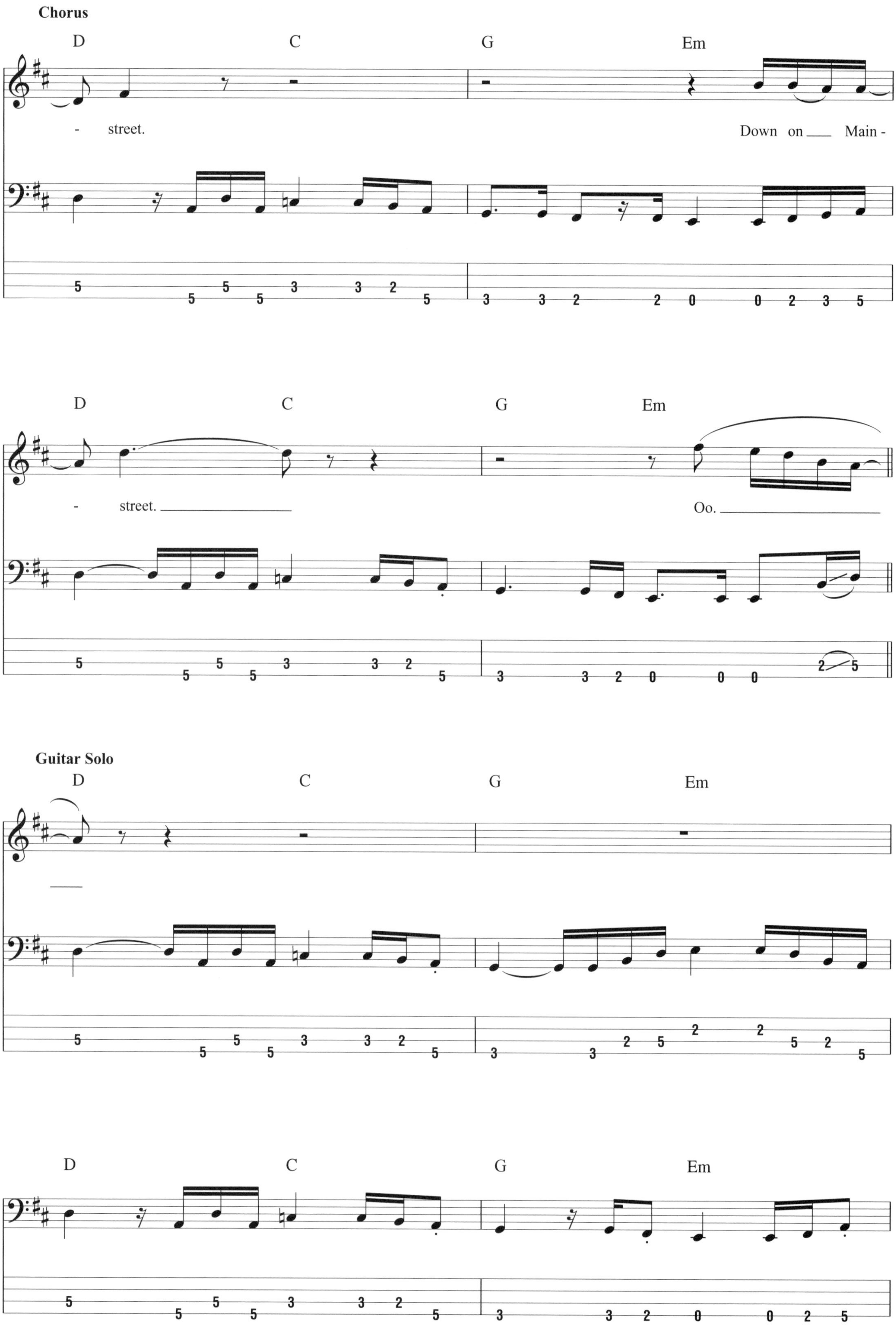

Chorus

D C G Em

\- street. Down on Main -

D C G Em

\- street. Oo.

Guitar Solo

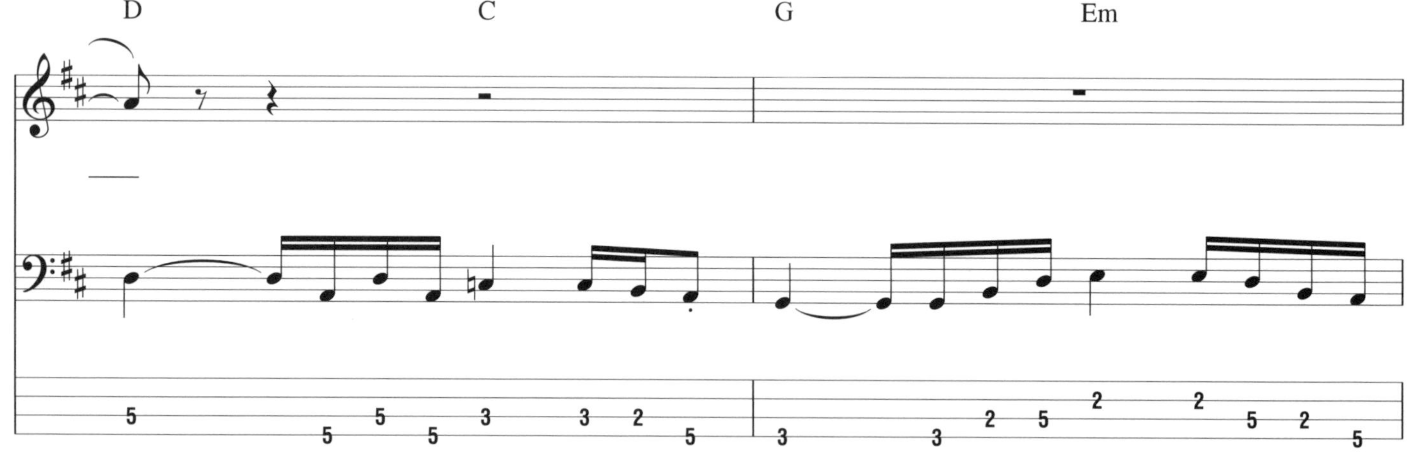

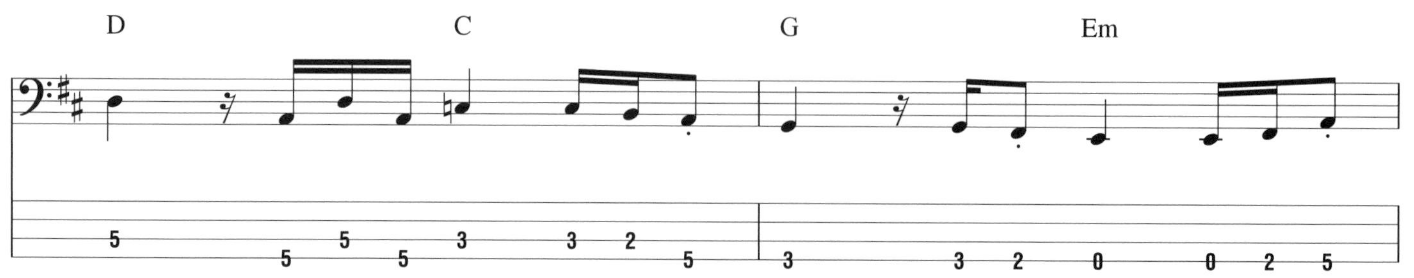

D
C
G
Em

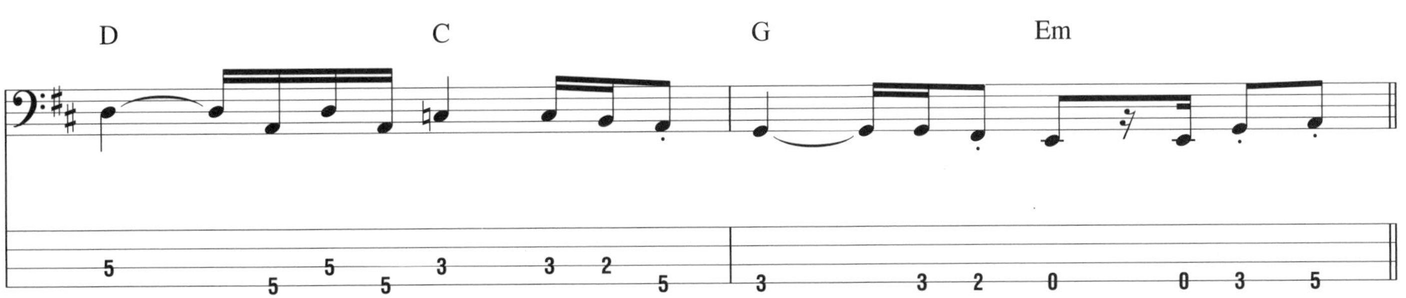
D
C
G
Em

Pre-Chorus
Bm
B9sus4
Bm
B9sus4
Some - times e - ven now, when I'm feel - ing lone - ly and beat.

F♯m
G
Em
G/A
I drift back in time and I find my feet down on Main -

Outro

D
Am
D
Am
- street.
Down on Main -
D
Am
D
Am
- street.
Down on Main -
D
Am
D
Am
- street.
Down on Main-
D
Am
D
Am
- street.
Down on Main-

D
Am
D
Am
- street.
Down on Main -

D
Am
D
Am
- street.

C
G
D

Old Time Rock & Roll

Words and Music by George Jackson and Thomas E. Jones III

F♯
rock and roll.
Don't try to take me to a dis - co.
You'll nev - er e - ven get me
B
out on the floor.
In ten min- utes, I'll be
To Coda
C♯
late for the door.
I like that old - time a
F♯
rock and roll.
Chorus
C♯
Still like that old - time a
F♯
rock and roll.
That kind of mu - sic just

B
C♯
soothes the soul.
I rem - i - nisce a - bout the days of old

F♯
C♯
with that old - time a rock and roll. Hey!

Guitar Solo

F♯
B

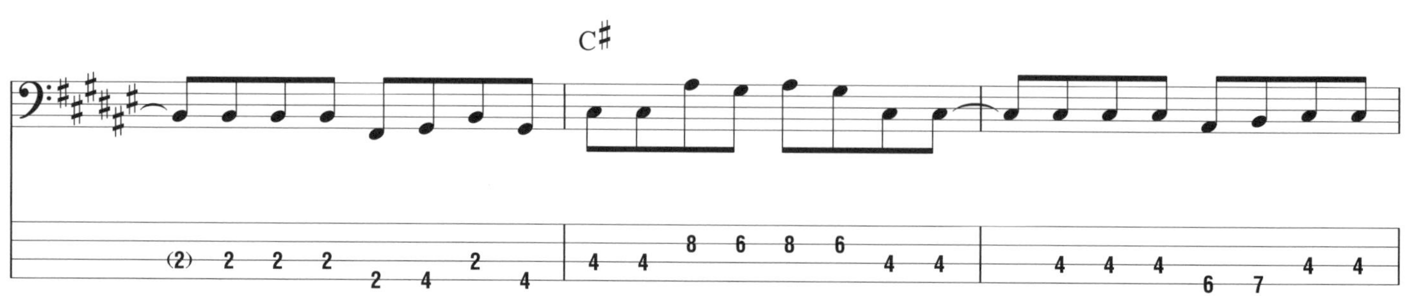
C♯

D.S. al Coda
F♯
C♯
2. Won't go to hear 'em play a
Coda
Chorus
C♯
F♯
Still like that old - time a rock and roll.
B
That kind of mu - sic just soothes the soul.
I rem - i - nisce a - bout the
C♯
F♯
days of old
with that old - time a rock and roll. Ow!

Saxophone Solo
C♯
F♯
B
C♯
F♯
C♯
Still like that old - time a
Chorus
F♯
B
rock and roll.
That kind of mu - sic just soothes the soul.
C♯
I rem - i - nisce a - bout the days of old
with that old - time a

F♯
C♯
rock and roll.
Still like that old - time a
Breakdown-Chorus
Bass tacet
N.C.
rock and roll.
That kind of mu - sic just soothes the soul.
I rem - i - nisce a - bout the days of old
with that old - time a
C♯
rock and roll.
Hey!
Still like that old - time a
Chorus
F♯
B
rock and roll.
That kind of mu - sic just soothes the soul.

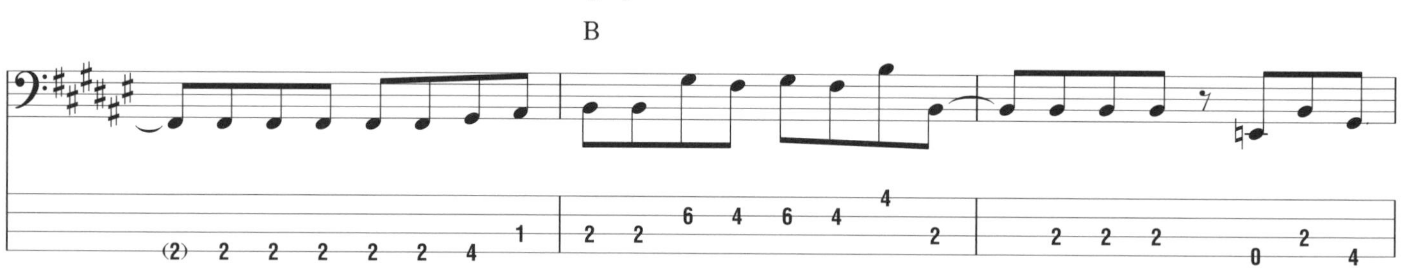

Additional Lyrics

2. Won't go to hear 'em play a tango.
   I'd rather hear some blues or funky old soul.
   There's only one sure way to get me to go:
   Start playing old time rock and roll.
   Call me a relic, call me what you will.
   Say I'm old-fashioned, say I'm over the hill.
   Today's music ain't got the same soul.
   I like that old time rock and roll.

Rock and Roll Never Forgets

Words and Music by Bob Seger

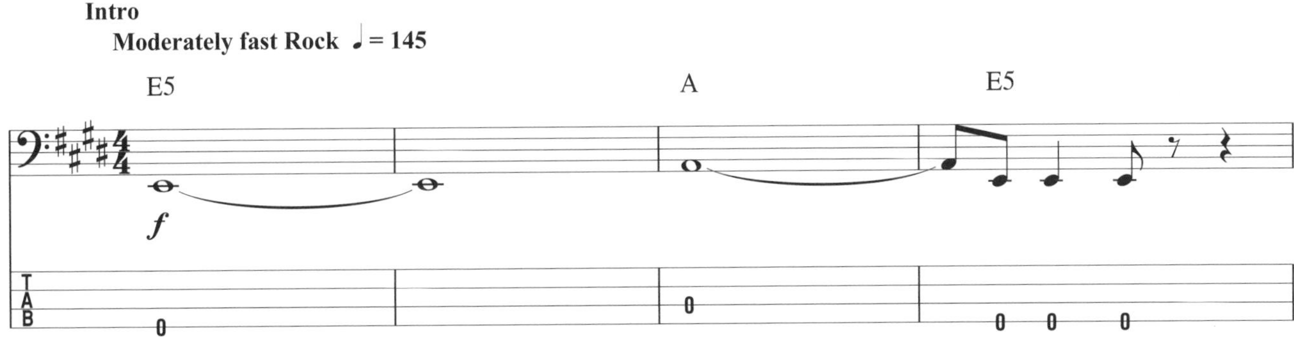

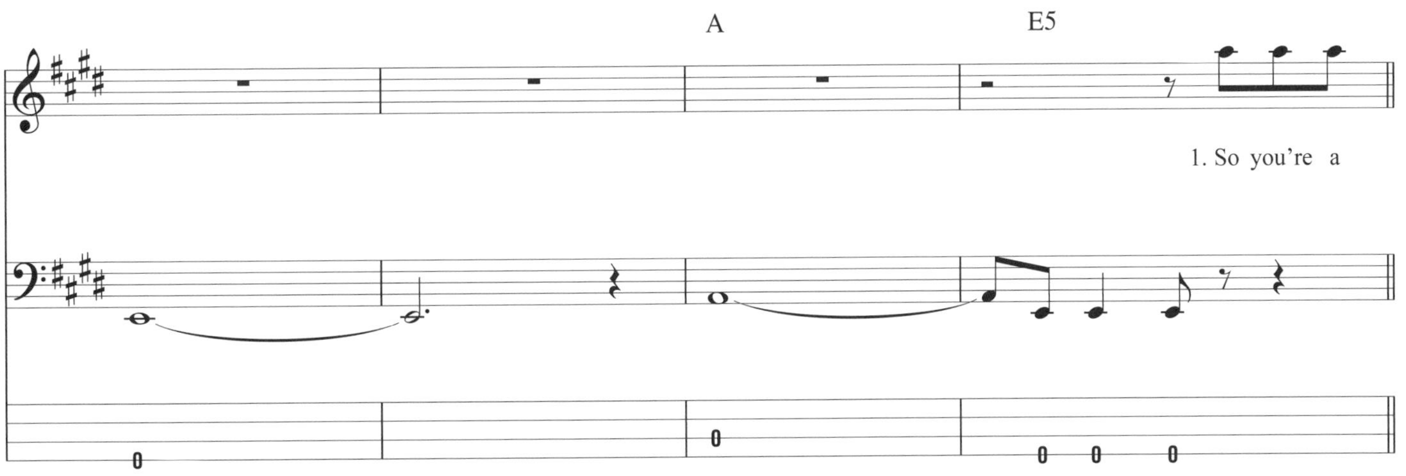

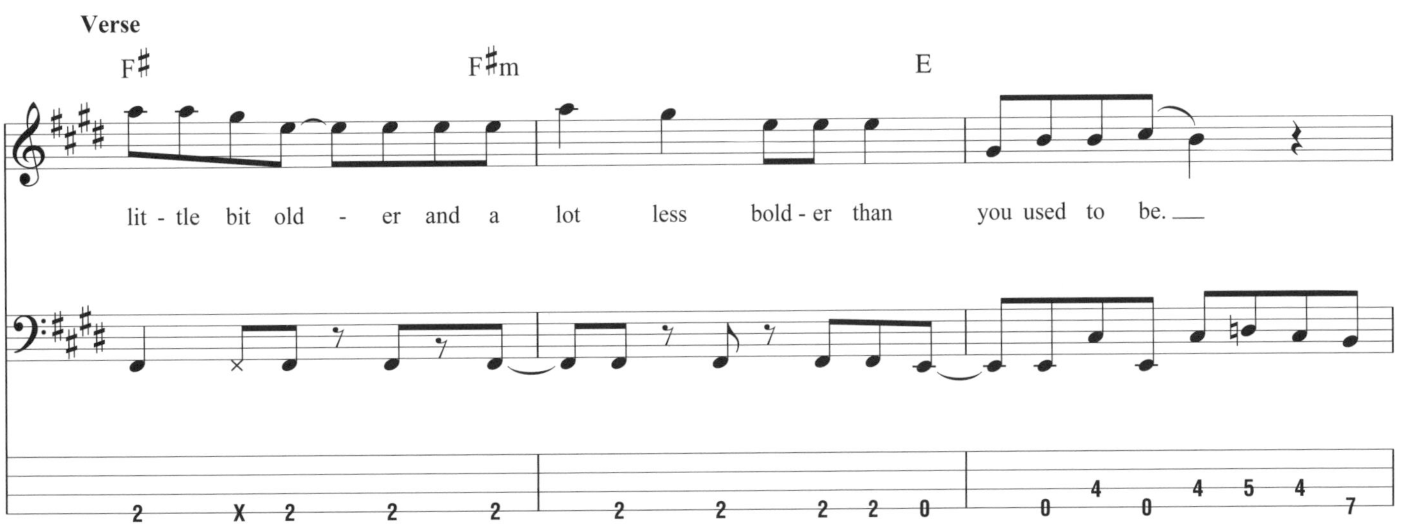

F♯
F♯m
E
So you used to shake 'em down, but now you stop and think a - bout your
Chorus
A
dig - ni - ty.
So, now sweet six - teen's turned
E
A
E
A
thir - ty - one, you get to feel - in' wear - y when the work day's done. Well, all
E
B5
you got to do is get up and in - to your kicks

F♯
if you're in a fix.
Come
F♯m
B
E
back, ba - by, rock and roll nev - er for - gets.
Verse
N.C.
F♯
F♯m
E
2. You bet - ter get your-self a part - ner, go down to the con - cert or the
F♯
F♯m
lo - cal bar.
Check the lo - cal news - pa - per; chanc-

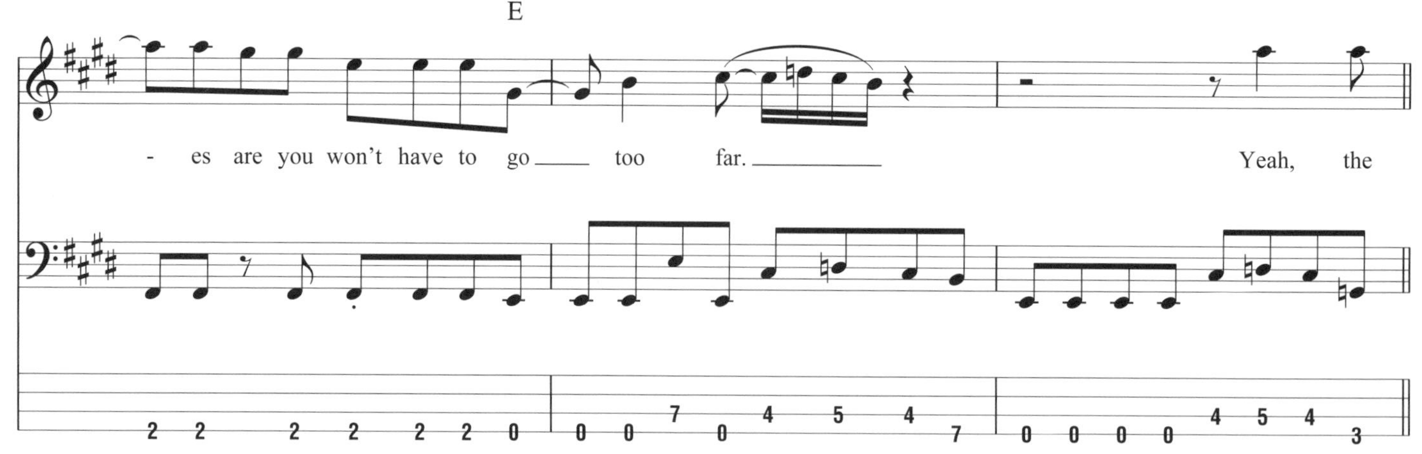
E
- es are you won't have to go too far. Yeah, the
2 2 2 2 2 2 0 0 0 7 0 4 5 4 7 0 0 0 0 4 5 4 3

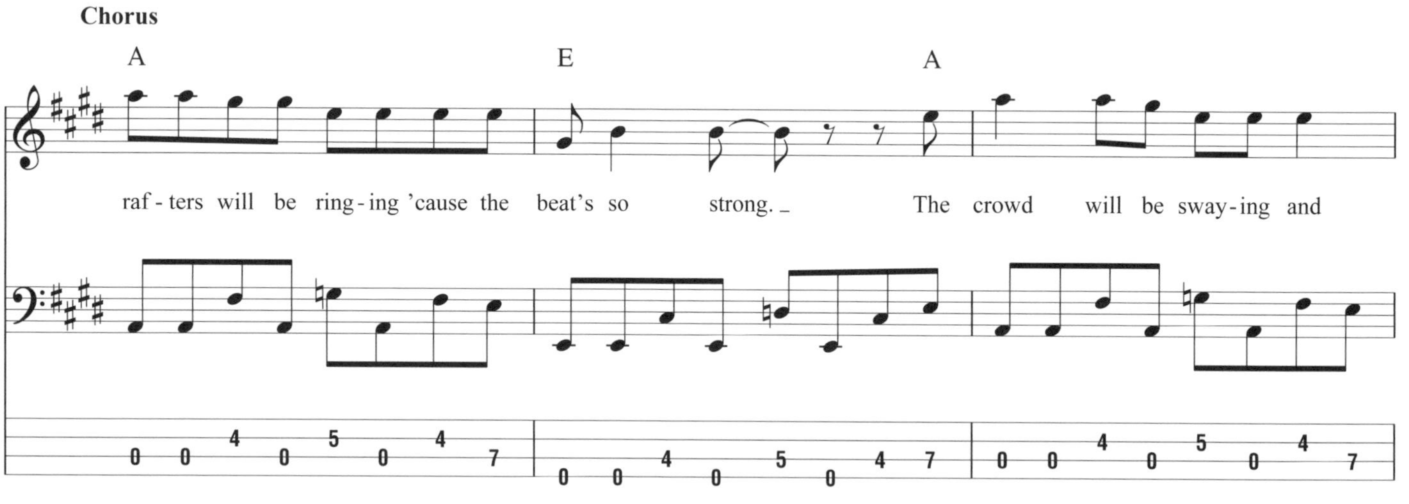
Chorus
A
E
A
raf - ters will be ring - ing 'cause the beat's so strong. The crowd will be sway - ing and
0 0 4 0 5 0 4 7 0 0 4 0 5 0 4 7 0 0 4 0 5 0 4 7

E
A
E
sing - ing a - long, and all you need to do is get in, in - to the mix
0 0 4 0 5 0 5 0 0 4 0 5 0 4 7 0 0 4 0 5 0 4 7

B5
F♯
if you need a fix.
7 7 7 7 7 7 7 7 7 7 7 7 7 7 7 7 2 2 X 2 2 2 X 2

F♯m
B
You can come back, ba - by, rock and roll nev - er for - gets.
E
N.C.
Bridge
A
Oo, the band's still play - ing it
E
A
E
A
loud and lean. Lis - ten to the gui - tar play - er mak - ing it scream. All
E
B
you got to do is just make that scene to - night.

Hey, _ to - night! _ Woo!

Guitar Solo

F♯ F♯m E

F♯ F♯m E

Chorus

A

Well, now sweet six - teen's turned

E A E A

thir - ty - one. _ Feel a lit - tle tired, feel - ing un - der the gun. _ Well, all _

E
B5
of Chuck's children are out there, playing his licks.
F♯
Get into your kicks, then come
F♯m
B
E
back, baby, rock and roll never forgets.
F♯m
B
Said you can come back, baby, rock and roll never forgets.

E
F♯m
B
Oh, come back, ba - by, rock
0 0 4 0 7 7 4 7
0 0 4 0 7 7 4 7
2 X 2 2 2 4 2
E
N.C.
and roll nev - er for - gets.
Oo.
(2) 2 2 2 2 2 2
0 0 4 4 2 2 4 2
2
Interlude
E5
A
E5
Oh, yeah. Oh, yeah.
0
0
0 0 0
A
E5
Ha. Uh, huh. Uh, huh. Nev - er for - gets.
0
0
0 0 0

E
A
E
Oh,
no.
Oh,
no.
Oh,
0 0 4 0 5 0 4 7
0 0 4 0 4 5 4 7
0 0 4 0 5 0 4 7
A
nev - er for - gets.
Ah,
yeah.
Oo.
0 0 4 0 5 0 4 7
0 0 4 0 5 0 4 7
0 0 4 0 5 0 4 7
Outro-Guitar Solo
E
E
Oh,
Lord.
Hey!
0 0 4 0 5 0 4 7
0 0 4 0 5 0 3 2 2
0 0 4 0 5 0 4 7
A
E
Yeah!
Nev - er for - gets.
0 0 4 0 5 0 4 7
0 0 4 0 5 0 4 7
0 0 4 0 5 0 3 2 2

A
E
yeah.
Whoa,
whoa.
Oh,

A
oh,
oh,
oh,
oh,
oh.
Ah,
yeah.
Oo,

E
oo.
Ow!

A
E
Nev - er, nev - er for - gets.

A
E
Oh,
no.
Oh,
no.

A

Begin fade
E

A
E

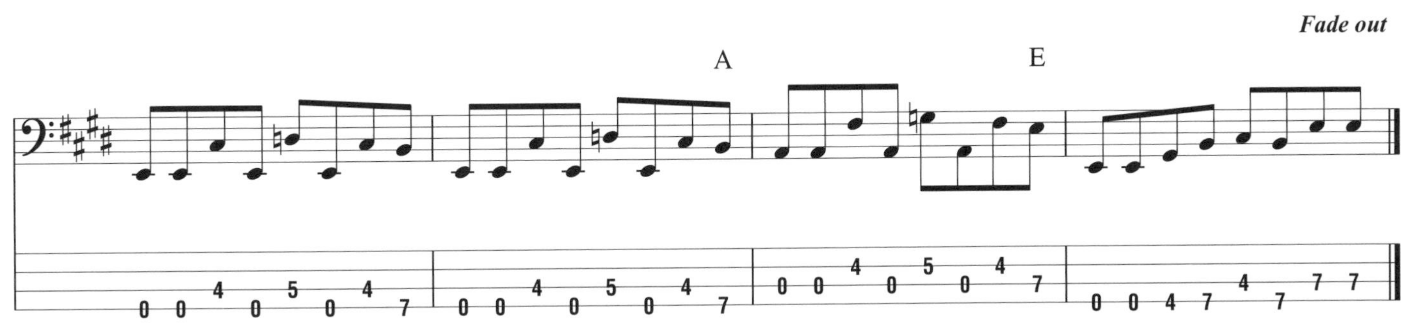
Fade out
A
E

HAL•LEONARD®

BASS PLAY-ALONG

AUDIO ACCESS INCLUDED

The Bass Play-Along™ Series will help you play your favorite songs quickly and easily! Just follow the tab, listen to the audio to hear how the bass should sound, and then play-along using the separate backing tracks. The melody and lyrics are also included in the book in case you want to sing, or to simply help you follow along. The audio files are enhanced so you can adjust the recording to any tempo without changing pitch!

1. Rock
00699674 .... $15.99

2. R&B
00699675 .... $15.99

3. Pop/Rock
00699677 .... $16.99

5. Funk
00699680 .... $16.99

6. Classic Rock
00699678 .... $16.99

7. Hard Rock
00699676 .... $16.99

9. Blues
00699817 .... $16.99

10. Jimi Hendrix Smash Hits
00699815 .... $17.99

11. Country
00699818 .... $12.95

12. Punk Classics
00699814 .... $12.99

13. The Beatles
00275504 .... $16.99

14. Modern Rock
00699821 .... $14.99

15. Mainstream Rock
00699822 .... $14.99

16. '80s Metal
00699825 .... $16.99

17. Pop Metal
00699826 .... $14.99

18. Blues Rock
00699828 .... $14.99

19. Steely Dan
00700203 .... $16.99

20. The Police
00700270 .... $17.99

21. Metallica: 1983-1988
00234338 .... $19.99

22. Metallica: 1991-2016
00234339 .... $19.99

23. Pink Floyd – Dark Side of The Moon
00700847 .... $15.99

24. Weezer
00700960 .... $14.99

25. Nirvana
00701047 .... $16.99

26. Black Sabbath
00701180 .... $16.99

27. Kiss
00701181 .... $16.99

28. The Who
00701182 .... $16.99

29. Eric Clapton
00701183 .... $15.99

30. Early Rock
00701184 .... $15.99

31. The 1970s
00701185 .... $14.99

32. Cover Band Hits
00211598 .... $16.99

33. Christmas Hits
00701197 .... $12.99

34. Easy Songs
00701480 .... $16.99

35. Bob Marley
00701702 .... $17.99

36. Aerosmith
00701886 .... $14.99

37. Modern Worship
00701920 .... $14.99

38. Avenged Sevenfold
00702386 .... $16.99

40. AC/DC
14041594 .... $16.99

41. U2
00702582 .... $16.99

42. Red Hot Chili Peppers
00702991 .... $19.99

43. Paul McCartney
00703079 .... $17.99

44. Megadeth
00703080 .... $16.99

45. Slipknot
00703201 .... $16.99

46. Best Bass Lines Ever
00103359 .... $17.99

47. Dream Theater
00111940 .... $24.99

48. James Brown
00117421 .... $16.99

49. Eagles
00119936 .... $17.99

50. Jaco Pastorius
00128407 .... $17.99

51. Stevie Ray Vaughan
00146154 .... $16.99

52. Cream
00146159 .... $17.99

56. Bob Seger
00275503 .... $16.99

57. Iron Maiden
00278398 .... $17.99

HAL•LEONARD®

Visit Hal Leonard Online at **www.halleonard.com**

Prices, contents, and availability subject to change without notice.

0319
334

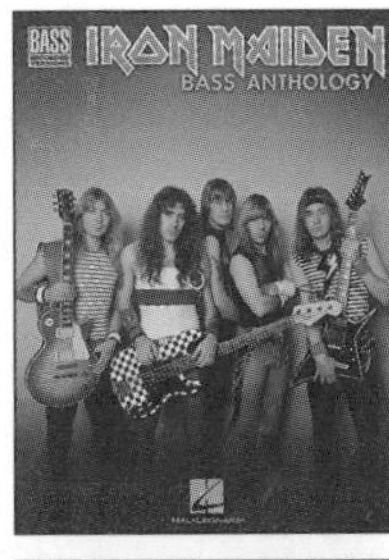

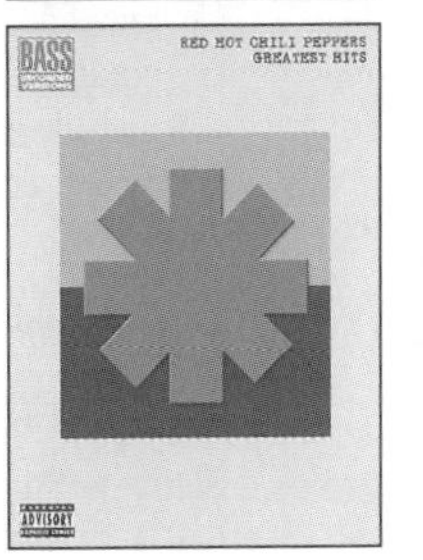

Bass Recorded Versions feature authentic transcriptions written in standard notation and tablature for bass guitar. This series features complete bass lines from the classics to contemporary superstars.

25 Essential Rock Bass Classics
00690210 / $17.99

Avenged Sevenfold – Nightmare
00691054 / $19.99

Bass Tab White Pages
00690508 / $29.99

The Beatles – Abbey Road
00128336 / $22.99

The Beatles Bass Lines
00690170 / $14.95

The Beatles 1962-1966
00690556 / $19.99

The Beatles 1967-1970
00690557 / $22.99

The Best of Blink 182
00690549 / $18.95

Best of Bass Tab
00141806 / $15.99

Blues Bass Classics
00690291 / $17.99

Boston Bass Collection
00690935 / $19.95

Stanley Clarke Collection
00672307 / $19.99

Dream Theater Bass Anthology
00119345 / $24.99

Funk Bass Bible
00690744 / $24.99

Hard Rock Bass Bible
00690746 / $19.99

Jimi Hendrix – Are You Experienced?
00690371 / $17.95

Jimi Hendrix Bass Tab Collection
00160505 / $22.99

Iron Maiden Bass Anthology
00690867 / $22.99

Jazz Bass Classics
00102070 / $17.99

Best of Kiss for Bass
00690080 / $19.95

Lynyrd Skynyrd – All-Time Greatest Hits
00690956 / $19.99

Bob Marley Bass Collection
00690568 / $19.99

Mastodon – Crack the Skye
00691007 / $19.99

Megadeth Bass Anthology
00691191 / $19.99

Metal Bass Tabs
00103358 / $19.99

Best of Marcus Miller
00690811 / $24.99

Motown Bass Classics
00690253 / $16.99

Muse Bass Tab Collection
00123275 / $19.99

Nirvana Bass Collection
00690066 / $19.99

No Doubt – Tragic Kingdom
00120112 / $22.95

The Offspring – Greatest Hits
00690809 / $17.95

Jaco Pastorius – Greatest Jazz Fusion Bass Player
00690421 / $19.99

The Essential Jaco Pastorius
00690420 / $19.99

Pearl Jam – Ten
00694882 / $17.99

Pink Floyd – Dark Side of the Moon
00660172 / $15.99

The Best of Police
00660207 / $17.99

Pop/Rock Bass Bible
00690747 / $17.95

Queen – The Bass Collection
00690065 / $19.99

R&B Bass Bible
00690745 / $19.99

Rage Against the Machine
00690248 / $19.99

The Best of Red Hot Chili Peppers
00695285 / $24.95

Red Hot Chili Peppers – Blood Sugar Sex Magik
00690064 / $19.99

Red Hot Chili Peppers – By the Way
00690585 / $22.99

Red Hot Chili Peppers – Californication
00690390 / $19.99

Red Hot Chili Peppers – Greatest Hits
00690675 / $19.99

Red Hot Chili Peppers – I'm with You
00691167 / $22.99

Red Hot Chili Peppers – One Hot Minute
00690091 / $19.99

Red Hot Chili Peppers – Stadium Arcadium
00690853 / $24.95

Red Hot Chili Peppers – Stadium Arcadium: Deluxe Edition
Book/2-CD Pack
00690863 / $39.95

Rock Bass Bible
00690446 / $19.99

Rolling Stones
00690256 / $17.99

Royal Blood
00151826 / $22.99

Slap Bass Bible
00159716 / $19.99

Sly & The Family Stone for Bass
00109733 / $19.99

Best of Billy Sheehan
00173972 / $24.99

Best of Yes
00103044 / $19.99

Best of ZZ Top for Bass
00691069 / $22.99

Visit Hal Leonard Online at
www.halleonard.com

Prices, contents & availability subject to change without notice.
Some products may not be available outside the U.S.A.